PROSPECT OR PREDATOR

The Real Estate Agent's Guide to Personal Safety

GARY VAN CLIEF

PROSPECT OR PREDATOR
The Real Estate Agent's
Guide to Personal Safety

© Copyright 2019

All Rights Reserved. No part of this book may be reproduced, distributed, or transmitted in any form or by any means without prior written permission form the copyright owner.

ISBN: 9781090881823

4CMLML

CONTENTS

1. Time After Time 1
2. The Perfect Victim 11
3. A Wolf in Sheep's Clothing 21
4. Liar Liar 31
5. The Sixth Sense 45
6. Situational Awareness 53
7. On the Road Again 65
8. Open House 79
9. Show and Tell 89
10. Information Security 97
11. Tech Talk 109
12. Friends 117
13. Stalking 129
14. The Office 141
15. Active Shooter 153
16. The Mindset of Self-Protection 163
17. The Fundamentals of Self-Protection 175
18. The Tactics of Self-Protection 183
19. Armed and Dangerous 195
20. Red Hot Chili Peppers 209
21. The Fox and the Old Lion 217

PROSPECT OR PREDATOR

"We hope all danger may be overcome; but to conclude that no danger may ever arise would itself be extremely dangerous."
- Abraham Lincoln

TIME AFTER TIME — 1

By lunchtime, the news had circulated throughout the office and a somber mood lingered in the air like a morning fog. The story was on everyone's minds and lips, and the sketchy details of what had actually happened varied depending upon who you spoke to. There was some talk of an angry ex, and a few just referred to it as a random crime, but as more information emerged it seemed that neither was the case. Much would be learned about the victim and the assailant over the coming days and weeks, but at that time only one thing was known for sure. A real estate agent in a neighboring county had been brutally raped and murdered, all while doing nothing more than showing a property to a potential buyer.

It was the number one topic of conversation at Hometown Realty that day and would remain so for some time to come. The agents in this small suburban office were a close-knit group, and although they had never met the victim, this tragedy seemed to resonate with each and every one of them. Perhaps it was the proximity, only about an hour's drive away on the interstate, that struck such a painful chord. The daily news coverage made it hard to ignore as this sad story literally hit "too close to home". It wasn't the first time they had heard about a real estate agent falling victim to crime, not by a long shot. Just last month there had even been a story featured on Dateline, and while the circumstances sounded eerily familiar, that was something that happened elsewhere, certainly not here.

More so than simple geography was the disturbing fact that this unfortunate agent was just like any one of them. She was a wife, a mother, a friend, and a colleague. She was an avid runner and a member of the PTA. Just an ordinary person living an ordinary life. The agents all struggled to understand what had happened, or more importantly why it had happened, and collectively hung on every new detail as it was released. Not out of a sense of morbidness mind you, but in an attempt to understand what fatal mistake had been made. What miscalculation had cost this poor woman her life?

In the end, that detail never came. By all accounts, there was no fatal mistake, no lapse in judgment. She wasn't reckless or careless and did nothing unusual that contributed to her demise. She simply crossed paths with the wrong person, a predator who thought nothing of harming her and ruthlessly taking her life. It would be so much easier if there had been that one critical error, that one deadly miscalculation upon which this entire story hinged. It's what people grapple with at times like these in a futile attempt to make sense of something that seems so senseless. We all do it. We scour through a sea of seemingly familiar details in search of that one inconsistency, one thing that we can point to and say, "I would never have done that" and by extension, "that could never happen to me".

As a real estate agent, it's probably safe to say that you are somewhat aware of the unique exposure that you face in your chosen profession. If you have not given serious consideration to those vulnerabilities, you should have at least taken notice of the efforts made by the realty industry as a whole to remind you to take precautions and to always protect yourself. Your National Association of REALTORS® recognizes the risks faced by its members and has dedicated every September as REALTOR® Safety Month. They have produced training videos and a great deal of printed material on the subject reminding agents to be ever vigilant and to make safety a priority in their professional lives.

For the agents at Hometown Realty, that's exactly what they did. They weren't about to take a passive approach to something so important as their own personal safety. Almost immediately the conversation turned from what had happened to what could be done. Safety checklists and articles were printed and distributed, sales meeting topics included the merits of the buddy system, and crime prevention literature adorned every bulletin board. Of course, their managing broker was all in and even had the Chief of Police give a talk as part of the lunch and learn program. A great deal was accomplished in those first few weeks and they all felt incredibly proud of just how much a highly motivated and mobilized group of agents could accomplish in a short period of time. "BE SAFE" became the mantra of the office and agents could regularly be heard reminding each other of just that.

And so the cycle begins... again.

It happens time after time, and the ensuing sequence of events is so predictable that you can practically set your watch by it. The catalyst is always a tragic event like the one described above, and just like the stages of grief, a series of emotions and reactions follow. First, there is shock and the accompanying fear that we might meet with a similar fate. Whenever we hear of tragedy striking someone that we share certain traits with, we can't help but think of ourselves and how "that could have been me". It may seem a bit self-centered but it's a natural response and a reminder of our own mortality. Some might think that the period of heightened awareness that follows this type of tragedy is a positive thing, but it tends to border on paranoia, and for a while, everyone is viewed with suspicious eyes. While agents may feel safer during that time, living life filled with anxiety and mistrust isn't at all healthy, and quite frankly, it gets in the way of productivity. If you are projecting that you do not trust your clients, how are they to be expected to trust you with what may be the most important financial transaction of their lives? Putting productivity aside for the moment, much like a fad diet, extreme measures that may well be effective are simply not sustainable.

As time passes, so does the memory of something that everyone would much rather forget. The crime prevention posters are now buried under fliers for continuing education classes, and the catchphrase "be safe" has gone the way of other outdated cliches. The incident isn't really discussed around the office anymore aside from the annual reminders during REALTOR® Safety Month. It's a common cycle that begins with overreaction and ends with a return to complacency. People tend to block out that which makes them uncomfortable or causes distress, often choosing a false sense of security over the real thing. But I can assure you that this view of your work life through rose-colored glasses is temporary as the clock is most certainly ticking and counting down to the day when tragedy inevitably strikes, and the cycle begins again.

While this all might sound rather foreboding, that is certainly not the intent of this book. My objective is to empower not to frighten, but to successfully combat danger we must at least be willing to look it squarely in the eye. One of the most consistent objections I hear regarding personal safety is the staunch refusal to live one's life in fear, and to be honest, it's a valid argument. Perhaps the greatest challenge in the realm of security is to overcome the misconception that self-protection can only be accomplished by way of fear and paranoia. For our purposes, and in the context of safety for the real estate professional, security can also be viewed as somewhat of a nuisance and overall, as a hindrance to success and profitability. I write this book with the belief that safety and productivity need not compete. To the contrary, being armed with knowledge and a new set of skills will not only keep you safe but result in a heightened level of awareness and confidence that can actually enhance your success as an agent.

Now I am certainly not the first person to broach the subject of safety and security for real estate agents. Aside from the information put out by various industry organizations, countless books and articles have been written on the topic over the years. Unfortunately, all of the material that I have come across is grossly inadequate and usually falls into two basic categories. The first is the generic personal safety information that fails to take into account the very specific and unique risks faced by agents. A few sentences will be added here and there and a handful of words will be changed in an attempt to tailor the work towards the realty business. The second type leans to the opposite extreme and is very industry specific but usually does more to point out the risks that you are already well aware of than to address those risks and offer practical ways to combat them. These works are generally written by well-meaning real estate professionals who are all too familiar with the dangers that exist but simply lack the security and self-protection expertise to outline an effective yet unobtrusive approach to personal safety.

Aside from being incredibly incomplete, the vast majority of information available to the agent today has not changed nor has it been updated in decades. Safety tips recommending the most basic precautionary measures like the "buddy system" and to "always wear your ID badge" are elementary at best and leave agents lacking the skills to effectively protect themselves. Just as the real estate industry has evolved over the years, so have the efforts of those who are willing to harm you. While technology and the internet specifically have created new and exciting opportunities for the real estate professional, those same technological advances have opened new doors for the criminal element. We live in an increasingly violent society, and the exposure faced by real estate agents has never been greater. Statistics show that attacks against agents, although usually isolated occurrences, have become increasingly common while many more incidents go unreported each year.

I wholeheartedly assert that this text is something different, something that goes above and beyond. I set out to create a comprehensive resource for the real estate agent that will cover every aspect of safety and security as it pertains to your career. Prevention is obviously the most important element of any safety and security program, and much of this book is devoted to just that, but while most materials focus heavily on avoidance they fail to address effective measures that go a step further. It is not enough to prevent and avoid, you must also learn the skills required to recognize, to escape, and to combat a threat if necessary. It may be true that an ounce of prevention is worth a pound of cure, but we can't ignore the fact that sometimes, and often through no fault of our own, the unthinkable happens.

As a real estate agent, I'm guessing that your personal safety is something that you have been forced to consider at one time or another, whether you've wanted to or not. Aside from stating the obvious fact that you are currently reading this book, more than likely you have been reminded of your own vulnerability as an agent on more than one occasion. Maybe you know of someone who was victimized or have heard a story similar to the one characterized in this chapter. Perhaps you have simply been in a situation where you felt uncomfortable while alone with a client. Whatever the case may be, you know all too well that your everyday activities as a real estate agent can leave you alone, isolated, and exposed to danger.

While that information may be common knowledge among you and your co-workers, most people outside of the industry don't realize the inherent risk that goes along with being a real estate agent. Even the idea of this book was often met with, "safety and security for real estate agents...?", a puzzled look contorting their faces. To be honest, there was a time when this topic caught me a bit off guard as well. It was something that I just hadn't given much thought to. That was forever changed by a conversation I had with my real estate agent some years back. As I recall, it all began with a simple request and one that I was more than happy to oblige.

THE PERFECT VICTIM   2

The car snaked along the gentle curves of South Tropical Trail following the naturally irregular shoreline of the Banana River. It was a picture-perfect morning on Merritt Island, 78 degrees, clear skies, and the water was flat and glassy. I couldn't help but think to myself that this was not bad for mid-January, not bad at all. Florida still seemed new to me then and continued to feel like a bit of an adventure. It was my second year in the Sunshine State since fleeing the Northern climes of New Jersey, leaving the harsh winters as well as my previous life far behind.

I had spent the last several years working as a security consultant covering the area in and around New York City. I enjoyed the work, but it also offered the flexibility to pursue another passion, real estate. I first cut my teeth on a 1923 Craftsman-style bungalow in the suburbs of Bergen County. The house had "good bones" as they say, not to mention some great character. The chestnut trim, stained glass windows, brick fireplace, and original hardwood floors were all great selling features, but the house was also in considerable disrepair and in the midst of foreclosure. The dormered attic had been converted to an apartment, and although it needed to be completely renovated, the prospect of rental income to offset the mortgage payment was more than enough reason to take the risk. Of course the project had its ups and downs, as I'm sure any first time rehabber can relate, but in the end, it was a success. The neighbors were thrilled to see the house looking good again, the value increased, and the monthly rent check was enough to make me feel like I might actually know what I was doing. Yep, I was hooked.

Now 1100 miles to the south and a handful of properties later, I was on my way to look at more distressed real estate that no one else wanted anything to do with. Keep in mind that this was back before the bubble changed everything and even the worst houses began selling for outrageous amounts, often well above list price. Settled into the passenger seat and quietly thumbing through a stack of MLS printouts was Lynn, my partner in crime so to speak, also known as my real estate agent. Lynn found my first foreclosure house when I moved to Florida and we had become fast friends. We've been through countless adventures since, the likes of which could probably fill up a few chapters all on their own, but I'll save those stories for another day. It's now many years later, but I can still hear the sound of Lynn laughing uncontrollably when she found me wedged midway through a doggy door hoping to get a look at the inside of an abandoned house.

I've always liked the challenge of a fixer-upper and the nastier it looked, the better. My niece, who was about 8 at the time, once asked "Why does Uncle Gary always buy such ugly houses"? The way I looked at it, if I was going to gut half the house anyway, it might as well be in really horrendous shape, thus eliminating competition from the faint of heart and essentially lowering the amount that a motivated seller might accept. Lynn had a talent for finding those diamonds in the extreme rough, and although I had acquired my Florida agent's license, it remained inactive and more often than not, I deferred to her years of experience and vast knowledge of the market.

Our most recent escapade had been a great little four bedroom 2 bath Rutenberg split in a very desirable neighborhood in Merritt Island. The house was free and clear and the taxes were up to date. The woman who owned it had simply, and apparently quite suddenly, decided to up and move. The only problem was that she had done so more than 9 years earlier. Strangely, the house wasn't even up for sale. Lynn had stumbled across it and after tracking down the owner, I made a cash offer. The house was left filled with old furniture and all kinds of personal belongings, not to mention a great deal of filth and evidence that rats had been the most recent occupants. There was clothing in the washing machine and even food left in the refrigerator. I can remember hesitantly opening it and thinking of that Geraldo special where he opened Al Capone's vault. The house was surreal, a time capsule of sorts, but after a great deal of work it turned out to be a very profitable flip.

On this gorgeous day, as it turned out, our efforts would not be quite so fruitful. None of the properties that we checked out were good candidates to be my next adventure, but I always love looking at property and trying to see the potential through the mess. At the very least, it was a nice day for a drive in the company of a good friend. What made this outing different, and the reason that it is still so memorable, was the conversation that took place on the return trip. It really struck a chord with me and the thoughts that it provoked have been with me ever since. I've spent quite a bit of time over the years considering the seriousness of that conversation and I can say with absolute certainty that it was the catalyst for the book that you are reading right now.

I was lost in thought at the moment, probably wondering where we should stop off for lunch, when Lynn broke the silence.

"Would you mind coming with me on my next appointment?"

"Sure." I replied, giving the question some thought. "Why, what's up?"

"I'm meeting this client… I don't know, just something about him I guess." Lynn answered.

I pondered what she had said for several moments before inquiring; "Does that happen often?"

Lynn went on to tell me how safety was a very real concern among those who worked in real estate and was especially so for female agents. Being alone with clients, entering empty and sometimes vacant houses, and showing properties in very isolated or rural areas were all in a day's work for a hard-working real estate agent. She even mentioned one agent that I knew personally who carried a gun on every one of her appointments. This all came as a complete surprise to me, and to be honest, I was a little embarrassed to admit that. After all, I had spent the better part of the last fifteen years protecting others and teaching others to protect themselves. In my defense, I had stepped away from that part of my life, and my shift in focus to real estate was a deliberate one. Until that moment, I hadn't considered the unique dangers that were faced by real estate agents. I just never really gave it much thought.

As is often the case, once you take notice of something it not only seems incredibly obvious in retrospect, but the reminders of that fact seem to pop up at every turn. I started to become acutely aware each time an incident was reported on the news or in the paper and even saw stories featured on programs like Dateline and 20/20. It soon became quite apparent that real estate agent safety was an extremely serious issue and what's more, the circumstances of each case had certain key elements that played perfectly into a criminal's hands. At the very core of the problem was the simple fact that the everyday activities of a real estate agent mesh all too well with what a predator seeks when selecting a victim.

The first and probably most critical factor is that real estate agents usually work alone. Even those who are partnered with another agent will often operate independently from each other. For obvious reasons, the most important thing that a criminal will look for is a lone victim. A single person is much easier to control and overpower than multiple victims. Even if the assailant is overly large or strong, it is still far more difficult to corral two victims than one.

The next thing a criminal will desire is privacy. He must have seclusion to carry out his crime without detection and without any pesky good Samaritans coming to the aid of his victim. Just as a legitimate prospect will have certain things that they are looking for in a property, a predator will also have his own wish list. Vacant houses are sometimes described as such in the listing, but that fact can also be evident when viewing the online photos. Location is also a key factor for a criminal as properties in more remote locations or on large lots mean that the nearest neighbors may be well out of earshot.

A criminal whose intent is to steal is looking for a target that offers the best monetary payout for his efforts, someone wearing expensive jewelry or driving an expensive car, for example. Real estate agents, like anyone working in a sales environment, will understandably try to present themselves as not only well qualified but also as successful. A nice car, fine jewelry, and expensive electronics are all part of that professional image.

A sexual predator will usually have a very specific selection process as it pertains to his targets. Serial rapists and killers will often fixate on victims of the same gender, with the same hair color, or with similar physical characteristics. A professional headshot is almost always a part of a real estate agent's marketing materials and when it comes to photography, we all try to portray ourselves in the most favorable and flattering light. To the deviant mind, the agent photos found in real estate advertising can sadly be used as a virtual catalog of potential victims.

All of these factors make real estate agents disproportionately vulnerable to crime as compared to people working in other professions. Quite some time has now passed since that first conversation with Lynn, but I've never stopped pondering the dilemma of agent safety and security. I've spoken to many real estate professionals over the years about this very issue, asking questions and listening to their unique experiences. While they don't seem to dwell on it, they all give the impression that they are aware, to various degrees, of the risks that they face. What once caught me off guard now seemed so incredibly obvious. A real estate agent is, quite simply, as close to a perfect victim as any predator could ever hope for.

BY THE NUMBERS

33% of Real Estate professionals experienced a situation that made them fear for their personal safety or the safety of their personal information.

41% of female Real Estate professionals experienced a situation that made them fear for their personal safety or the safety of their personal information.

6% of Real Estate professionals were a victim of a crime (violent or not) while working.

43% of Real Estate professionals chose to carry some type of self-defense weapon.

Source: 2018 Member Safety Report - National Association of REALTORS®

> *"When he was away from being a compliance officer he was a great guy, excellent personality."*
>
> *- Donna Berry, neighbor of Dennis Rader aka the BTK Killer*

A WOLF IN SHEEP'S CLOTHING 3

We've been told since we were kids never to talk to strangers and to always beware of suspicious characters. As children, that vague advice seemed straightforward enough and not too difficult to follow. Now that we are adults, it's easier said than done. For starters, you make your living as a real estate agent by interacting with people and talking to strangers. As for suspicious characters, well... they can be rather difficult to spot unless, of course, you know what to look for. So what are the key indicators that a person may not be on the "up and up"? First and foremost, bad guys always wear dark clothing. That one's a given. Thanks to the motion picture industry, we know that anyone wearing a cloak or cape should be avoided at all costs. Facial hair, especially a five o'clock shadow or a pencil-thin mustache is also quite suspect. Now, I know these examples are deliberately absurd, but my obvious point is that the predators of the world do not always look like the villains we expect them to be.

If history has taught us anything, appearance is of no value as an indicator of a person's true nature or their ultimate intentions. In the late 1970s, Wayne Williams killed 28 people in what came to be known as the Atlanta Child Murders and shattered the stereotype that serial killers are typically Caucasian men. Aileen Wuornos, the killer of 7 men in Florida between 1989 and 1990, showed us that not all serial killers are male. A person's occupation, religious beliefs, or family background, also lack substantive value when evaluating a potential threat. The Green River Killer, Gary Ridgeway, was known to read the bible while on breaks at work. Dennis Rader, the BTK killer, was very active in his church as well as being a volunteer Boy Scout leader. And of course, by now, we have all heard what a nice, charismatic, young man Ted Bundy was.

The only logical conclusion to be drawn from this information is that a person's physical appearance, as well as every other stereotype out there, is of no use in judging their character or anticipating their actions. To rely on such information is not only prejudicial but can actually put you at greater risk. If you have a biased stereotype as to what constitutes a bad person, you will also have a predetermined idea as to what a good person might look like. A predator knows just as well as you do what society views as sinister and will go to great lengths to alter his appearance and portray himself as non-threatening.

So if a criminal will do his best to disguise his intentions, how then are we to spot him? First and foremost, we need to let go of our own prejudices and stereotypes. If you are shaking your head and saying to yourself that you are free of such narrow-minded thinking, you must face the fact that we all have certain pre-judgments ingrained deep within our psyches. To really begin to see people and read them, we have to start with a clear mind. We must discard our misconceptions, not just out of moral obligation, but as a matter of practicality. Every person whose intent you misread is a potential threat to your safety. Viewing people in terms of stereotypes has far more serious ramifications than offending a good-intentioned prospect. Considerably more dangerous than the innocent person whom you have been suspicious of is the predator who has successfully deceived you.

Beyond letting go of societal stereotypes, we must reacquaint ourselves with the lost art of paying attention. While that might seem like an over-simplification, being observant may not be so easily accomplished as one might hope. In today's fast-paced society, it's easy to fly from conference call, to sales meeting, to showing, to closing, without a moments pause to take a breath. Our lives have become so hectic that we can navigate the course of our workday on virtual auto-pilot. We do things without giving them much thought and often do several things at once. It's fondly referred to as multitasking, but the work completed is usually inferior to the output resulting from focus and forethought. As a real estate agent, you know the importance of slowing down and giving a prospect your undivided attention, but what is it that you are focused on? A good salesperson will always want to make eye contact and listen intently to their client, you may even scribble down a note or two. Unfortunately, it has become far too commonplace to look without seeing and to hear without really listening.

Throughout this book, I will be asking you to try to think like a criminal. To an honest and decent person, that may seem a rather arduous task, but in reality, it is not all that difficult. There's no need to go to a dark place and imagine yourself as someone who would think nothing of victimizing another person or take pleasure in the pain and suffering of others. People can only draw from their own experiences and I am assuming that type of mentality is not in your nature. The most basic way to think like a criminal is to consider his motive, his intention, and his objective. While the deviant mind may include some rather warped logic, most criminal's thought processes will share certain elements, none more prevalent than the desire to avoid being caught. Much of his preparation and planning will be devoted to just that.

It is important to remember that a crime against a real estate agent is a very targeted attack. The perpetrator is not a street mugger waiting in the shadows in hopes that an unsuspecting person will happen by. He has selected his victim and probably given that choice considerable forethought. If he has not chosen the individual specifically, he has at least chosen their occupation. To effectively carry out his crime, he will rely heavily on deception. He will play the role of someone that you will not perceive as a threat, relying on your preconceived stereotypes of what a harmless home-buyer might look like. That deception is critical to the success of his crime. He knows that by portraying himself as a well-qualified prospect, he also represents a commission check, and is counting on you to be somewhat blinded by your own ambition.

A lot can be learned from the mindset of a predator. He is well versed in the subject of human nature and will use it to his advantage. While I may be viewed by some as quite cynical, I do believe that human beings by nature are basically optimistic. We want to believe that people are good and mean us no harm. It is commonly evident in the victim's statements immediately following an assault. Time after time they will say that the warning signs were there or that they "knew something wasn't right". Unfortunately, people will go to great lengths to explain away what in retrospect seems rather obvious. Out of an abundance of danger signals, they will find the one explanation that will make everything alright, no matter how implausible that explanation might be. It's also the reason that victims often describe feeling foolish after the fact as they come to the realization that they truly "should have known better".

Up until this point, I have deliberately focused a great deal on what NOT to focus on, but that is only half of the equation. Clearly, the other half is to consider what we should be focusing on and to answer the question, "What exactly does a suspicious person look like?". Knowing what you now know about stereotypes, you're probably thinking that this is a very complicated question to answer, but it's not. To be honest, it is a trick question. In reality, there is no such thing as a suspicious person, only suspicious behavior, and that should always be your primary focus. You may find it to be a difficult shift in thinking as the concept of the suspicious person has been embedded in our consciousness since we were small children. A person's actions are a far more accurate barometer as to their true intent than any preconceived notions that we might have. To effectively assess an individual's mindset, the obvious starting point is to observe their behavior.

If you really want to get an interesting look at people reading people, just tune into the next World Series of Poker tournament on TV. There you'll see an unusual cast of characters, some hunched down in their chairs and looking more like the Unabomber than a professional gambler, complete with dark sunglasses and a hoodie. These card players know that their behavior can potentially tip off their opponent and literally cost them millions of dollars. They are experts at reading the behavior of others, and what they are looking for is known as a "tell". It's a subconscious twitch, a sniff, or a scratch, really anything that might indicate that a player is bluffing. Now, if you were under the impression that poker is a game of luck, you would be mistaken. It is a test of people reading skills. If you're still not convinced, consider this one fact. Every year, there are tens of thousands of entrants into the tournaments on the World Poker Tour, and each time, with few exceptions, the final table consists of the same ten or twelve players. Every year. That's some luck, huh?

Now, some books on personal safety will spend a great deal of time talking about the animal kingdom and how all species, including humans, will display aggressive behavior. A diver knows that when a shark turns its pectoral fins downward, it is a sign of aggression. A snake will rear its head back when it is about to strike, and I'm sure you've seen a dog snarl and show his teeth. It can be rather easy to interpret the danger signals in animals as they do not make any attempt at hiding their intentions. The same cannot be said of human beings. For our purposes, and when reading the behavior of people, being able to recognize the signs of aggression is less important than you might think. The simple reason is that once a person is showing signs of aggression, it is far too late for preventative measures and you would be better served by skipping directly to the chapters on self-protection.

So if we're not looking for signs of aggression then what type of behavior is it that we should be keeping an eye out for? You can tell a great deal about any person and their state of mind by simply observing their behavior. From a preventative standpoint, what you want to be on the lookout for are signs of deception and the subsequent nervousness that it causes. That is the type of behavior that, if recognized, will give you the opportunity to take steps to protect yourself. Just about every case of a crime against a real estate agent has shared one common trait - they all involved some form of deception. The desire of any criminal is to catch his victim off guard and to use that to his advantage. While that might conjure images of an assailant leaping out of the shadows, the element of surprise can also be achieved by way of simple deceit. If you believe that the person that you are interacting with is not a threat, you will be much easier to target and literally become a help to the perpetrator rather than a hindrance. This deception is a key component of his crime. While it is at the crux of the problem, it also holds the key to the solution. If we start by recognizing this deception and seeing through the subterfuge, we can take away a key advantage that every criminal is seeking.

If you find it difficult to observe people on a deeper level in an effort to get a read on them, there is an exercise that you can do to further develop these skills. Now I never said there wouldn't be any homework. Actually, it's not as tedious as it may sound. Think of it as advanced people watching. The next time you are sitting at Starbucks or eating alone at the food court, try putting down your smartphone and just observe the people around you. Believe me, it will be an eye-opening experience. Don't just observe the people, but make observations about them. Look at their body language and facial expressions and see what conclusions you can draw from them. Try to come up with one adjective to describe each person. Do it quickly and then move on to the next person. Early on, your descriptions will be more superficial, but try not to repeat them too often. In time, as you continually try to come up with new descriptions, you will find that they will start to have deeper meaning. You may start with simple adjectives like man, woman, fat, skinny, old, and young. As your skills improve, you will observe more detail and begin to see things like hurried, tired, frustrated, or angry.

Observing couples and the way in which they interact with one another can also be a rather interesting exercise. With a little practice, the subtle differences between first dates and long-term relationships will become quite clear. In time, and with a little patience, you will begin to see people through an entirely new lens.

LIAR LIAR 4

When I was a boy, my mother convinced me that if I lied, white spots would appear on my tongue. Okay, so maybe I wasn't the brightest kid, but I do remember fibbing in front of the bathroom mirror in an effort to confirm this rather outlandish claim. In my defense, I was probably about five years old, and my mother would never lie to me, right? It was a rather clever ploy on her part, if only it were true. Imagine being able to verify the truthfulness of any statement by simply asking to see someone's tongue. Of course, my mother knew that all she needed to do was ask that very question, and my response would provide the answer. The idea of the spotted tongue test may seem preposterous, but it's hard to argue with success. After all, her accuracy rate was a perfect 100%. There were many times that I was sent to my room after refusing to open my mouth, bewildered and dejected, and obviously betrayed by my own behavior once again.

Children tend to wear their hearts on their sleeves, and it follows that they are quite easy to read. Even when they seek to deceive, their efforts are usually quite transparent. As time goes on, people become more adept at hiding their emotions. For most, it's just a defense mechanism as we become more guarded with age. For a predator, his motives may be far more sinister, and he may have become quite proficient at disguising his true intentions. To add to the challenge, it is much more difficult to interpret the behavior of a stranger than that of someone with whom you are previously acquainted. The person that you are familiar with is a known quantity, therefore you have the benefit of understanding what his or her normal behavior is.

If you've never taken a polygraph exam, you have probably at least seen the basics of one portrayed on television at one time or another. The polygraph examiner will always start by asking a series of questions that he already knows the answer to. This is done to establish what is known as a "baseline". By asking yes or no questions like "Is your name John Doe?" or "Do you live at 123 First Street?", the examiner can observe the subject's physiological responses when they are answering honestly. Once that baseline has been established, differences can be noted when the subject is being less than truthful. For the real estate agent, there is little opportunity to observe baseline behavior as the people you are dealing with are usually strangers.

I cannot stress enough that deception is a key ingredient in the targeting of a real estate agent, and recognizing that deceit will go a long way towards avoiding a potentially dangerous situation. At this point, you're probably reading through this chapter and waiting with great anticipation for me to reveal the closely guarded secret of how to become a human lie detector. You know, the technique that only the top CIA operatives know about. Until now, of course. The truth is, there is no magic bullet, and anyone trying to tell you otherwise is… lying. People who claim that there is one simple Gotcha! trick that can expose any liar in an instant are usually trying to sell you something. In reality, there is no single thing that you can point to and say "AHA, he's lying". There are, however, many key indicators of dishonesty that are not that difficult to spot, but it's important to remember that no one indicator is proof positive that someone is lying. Instead, we must look for multiple signs, or "clusters", when attempting to assess a person's truthfulness.

Lying may come easier for some than others, but overall, being dishonest is at least somewhat stressful for most people. A true psychopath is the exception to this rule as they lack conscience and therefore will not feel the slightest bit of guilt or remorse regarding their deceit or their actions. Nevertheless, most criminals are not the cool and calculating masterminds that are portrayed on television. They are likely to be very uptight about their deception, not to mention the crime they are about to commit and potential penalties they will face if caught. That alone is enough to make many criminals quite nervous and the resulting discomfort can manifest itself in a variety of ways. Just as the "lie detector" measures respiration, heart rate, blood pressure, and perspiration, those same physiological responses can be apparent even without the aid of a polygraph machine. There are many common characteristics that should cause you to take notice, especially when several of those traits are evident. They should not be unfamiliar to you, as I'm sure you have seen these signs displayed by others in a variety of non-threatening situations. Aside from witnessing someone who seems on edge, more than likely you have experienced those same feelings yourself. The signs of nervousness present themselves similarly regardless of the cause, whether it be a criminal who is lying to you or an agent who is uncomfortable giving a presentation in front of a group. Think of a time when you were very nervous and try to recall how that physically made you feel. Understanding these emotions will help to make them more recognizable when you see them exhibited by others.

Signs of Nervousness

- Avoids eye contact, watery eyes, eyes darting around
- Labored breathing, heavy exhales, sighs
- Fidgety demeanor, can't keep still for too long, jumpy, on edge, fidgeting with objects or tugging at clothing, can't keep feet still, constantly moving about the room
- Perspiration around the neck and face, excessive sweating, sweaty palms apparent upon first handshake, continuously drying palms on clothing
- Becoming flushed (blushing) around the face and neck
- Nervous ticks, twitches, touching of the face (mouth, nose, ears) often when answering questions
- Erratic speech patterns, talking too fast or too slow, struggling to respond to questions that should be easy to answer

Many agents who have been victimized will often mention some of these indicators after the fact. They will commonly describe the perpetrator as seeming "nervous" or "on edge". Unfortunately, hindsight is 20/20, and they would have done well to take note of these warning signs at the onset. While all of these indicators can be a sign of nervousness and dishonesty, it is important to remember that there are also harmless explanations for each and every one of them. If you are showing houses in Tucson in July, a perspiring client may not be cause for concern. There are also a number of medical ailments that could explain a person's uneasiness, not to mention the fact that we all have our own quirks and idiosyncrasies. Some people are just socially awkward or lack solid communication skills. Look for the clusters, multiple signs that a person is uncomfortable, and things that just don't seem to fit.

As we discussed in the previous chapter, an attack on a real estate agent is almost always a premeditated crime, and it is carried out with planning and forethought. It's one of the great challenges when it comes to personal safety. The criminal has a plan and knows what is about to take place, whereas the victim is left to react and improvise. A great deal of a predator's preparation will be devoted to the story he will tell. Without that deception, an agent would never willingly allow themselves to be alone with him. While his cover story may be well rehearsed, it is impossible to anticipate every possible question, and the details may get rather vague once you get beyond the surface.

Simple conversation is the most effective tool when it comes to evaluating an individual's honesty, and as a salesperson, you should be well versed in the art of communication. A predator will use speech to deceive so the more he speaks, the greater the chance he will slip up. Now, you may be thinking that you don't want to pry, or worse yet, come off as if you are interrogating what in most cases will be a totally harmless home buyer. In reality, there are many reasons to engage a prospect in conversation, and most of them have absolutely nothing to do with safety. Your priorities as an agent should be to build rapport and to get a better understanding of your client's needs. In general, people will find it complimentary that you are taking an interest, and most will have no problem talking about themselves. Your questions will be no different and still be of an innocent nature, but the more a dishonest person talks, the greater the likelihood that they will falter.

There is a certain synchronization to the truth. It is effortless and comes naturally. The same cannot be said about a lie. You don't have to stop and think about the truth as it is much easier to recall than to create. Mark Twain has been famously misquoted as saying "If you tell the truth, you don't have to remember anything". This statement holds true, regardless of who actually said it. If you have children, I'm sure you have noticed that when pressed, their fibs become more obvious and are usually littered with plenty of "ums" and "uhs". Speaking of kids, do you remember as a child challenging someone to pat their head and rub their belly at the same time? It always seemed like it should be a lot easier than it was. The same can be said about the synchronization of speech. It can be challenging to remember and recite a fictitious narrative and nearly impossible to control your eyes and body movements at the same time. A person will often be animated and loose while telling the truth but tense up when they are being dishonest. When telling a lie, people have even been known to say the word "yes" but at the same time, subconsciously shake their head "no". Often a criminal will incorporate a great deal of truth into his cover story as it is much easier to recite than a total fabrication, but it will take considerably more effort to continue this deception if you ask questions that require greater detail. Again, an honest home buyer won't be put off by this, and they will usually welcome your interest.

Now that we have discussed the signs of nervousness as well as synchronization, let's take a look at the key elements of evaluating truthfulness, what I refer to as "The Four C's". Now, I'm not talking about shopping for diamonds (cut, clarity, color, and carat weight), sorry to disappoint. What I am referring to are Credibility, Context, Consistency, and Contradiction. When you consider them as they pertain to the people that you interact with, you should find that the dishonest people out there will usually stumble over one, if not more, of these "authenticators".

The first element to look at is credibility, and it can be established in a variety of ways. The easiest way that a person will be viewed as credible is if you know who they are. Perhaps you have been acquainted with them in the past, or as is often the case in real estate, they are known to someone that you know and trust. If you are meeting with the cousin of your good friend Liz because he is planning to move to town, that would certainly carry some weight in the credibility department. That's not to say that Liz's cousin might just be a raving lunatic, but you get the idea. It is not enough on its own, but it gets you part way there. If someone is known in the area, their reputation will lend to their credibility. While it is not uncommon for a person to be victimized by someone they know, crimes against real estate agents are generally perpetrated by strangers. For obvious reasons, a criminal will always want to remain anonymous, so being diligent in regards to pre-qualifying your prospect will require him to provide a driver's license and produce other identifying information. It's important to keep in mind that fake IDs and the like are easy to come by these days, but each step that you take is a step in the right direction.

Now, I know that I have emphasized the importance of abandoning stereotypes, but that's not to say you shouldn't use common sense when evaluating someone. If they want to look at an $850,000 home but show up in tattered clothing or driving a twenty-year-old jalopy, you would probably want to take notice. Sometimes, it may not be quite so obvious. As mentioned before, a predator knows what you are looking for in a legitimate client, and he will do his best to try to fit the bill. If you have a keen eye or an interest in fashion, you can tell the difference between that which is truly expensive and that which is designed to look expensive. I know an agent who can spot a fake Rolex with just a handshake. Apparently, the second hand on the real article moves fluidly and does not "tick" from second to second. So take notice of those whose claims lack supporting data. But all of that being said, there is an exception to every rule. Sam Walton, the billionaire founder of Walmart, drove a 1979 Ford F-150 pickup truck, and the vehicle was reportedly not in the best condition.

The second "C" that we need to consider is context. It's a word that we use quite a bit, but it is important to understand exactly what it means. According to the Oxford

Dictionary, context is described as follows: "the circumstances that form the setting for an event, statement, or idea, and in terms of which it can be fully understood". Everything that a person might say should be evaluated based on the current circumstances under which it was said. It is why I despise conducting any meaningful conversation by way of text message. There just isn't any way to get the full meaning of what is intended and too many opportunities to be misunderstood. Just about any statement can be considered completely normal or totally off the wall, depending on the context. If you and I were to walk into a nightclub and I said "this place is on fire!", you would rightly assume that it was a positive statement. On the other hand, if I were to make that very same statement while standing in front of a doorway that was billowing smoke, you would probably run for the exit. You should consider the context of everything that someone tells you. Additionally, inappropriate comments are always cause for concern. Some statements may be perfectly acceptable between two close friends or a husband and wife, for example, but very much out of place in the context of a professional meeting.

The next key, and perhaps the most important "C", is consistency. A deceitful person may be well practiced in their cover story but with enough conversation, the cracks will usually begin to show. They simply can't anticipate every question or have thought of every possible detail. The basic points of their narrative may be well thought out but the deeper you delve, the easier it will be to spot inconsistencies in their story. Facts or time frames might not jibe with one another. Keep the conversation going, and you will give them plenty of rope to trip themselves up if they are lying. Living in Florida, a place where everyone seems to be from somewhere else, I will often ask "where are you from originally?". It's a good conversation starter and a question that an honest person should have no hesitation in answering. Just that simple inquiry can open the door to a great deal of discussion. Remember, taking an interest in someone and engaging them in conversation is simply a matter of good people skills and will help to establish a positive rapport with your client. If you listen carefully, any inconsistencies will start to become very obvious.

Pushed to its furthest extreme, inconsistency will eventually become contradiction, the fourth and final "C". It's the moment when it becomes very clear that the facts just don't add up. If you pay close attention, you will hear many contradictory statements from those who are being less than honest. While many statements might be truthful on their own, often two statements cannot both be true. In simplest terms, the person in question is lying. Dishonest people will usually know when they have contradicted themselves, or at least be tipped off by your subtle but noticeable reaction. At this point, you may begin to see some of those signs of nervousness that we spoke about. If you feel that you have enough information to draw a conclusion, it's best not to press too much further. Just as a cornered animal will lash out, an exposed liar will become defensive and unpredictable.

We've covered many of the red flags that may indicate dishonesty, but you should never rely on any one of them to draw a conclusion. Always look for multiple signs. As I have said, there is a certain synchronization to the truth, but there is also a pattern to deception. Playing fast and loose with the truth doesn't always mean that your prospect is a predator in disguise. He may be lying in an effort to impress you, to flirt with you, or for a far more devious purpose. The motive of his deception is yet to be determined, but he is being dishonest, none the less, and not worthy of your trust. If you feel that someone is being less than truthful with you, use your judgment as far as what to do next. If in doubt, and even if you're not, take a friend or colleague with you. If you are really getting a bad vibe from someone, walk away. No commission check is worth your life. As always, trust your instincts, and don't hesitate to report someone who seems really "hinky" to the police. Most people will say, "Well, he didn't actually do anything wrong", but the information that you provide may be a small piece of a larger puzzle and wind up solving a past crime or better yet, preventing a future one.

THE SIXTH SENSE   5

Have you ever had a feeling that something was about to happen before it did? A gnawing suspicion that you just couldn't shake? Perhaps a sense of impending doom? Call it what you like, a premonition, a hunch, or intuition, but most people report having experienced just such a phenomenon at some point in their lives. It can be hard to put into words and is often described as just a "feeling of uneasiness". The explanations for such occurrences can range from the purely logical and scientific to the supernatural and downright preposterous. Now, I am not going to delve into a discussion of the paranormal here but prefer to take a serious look at instinct and what many within the law enforcement community commonly refer to as your "sixth sense". You will notice that I used the word "your" as I am of the belief that such intuitive abilities exist within each and every one of us, finely honed in some while lying ignored and dormant in others.

As living, breathing, creatures, we as human beings possess certain instincts. These traits were never taught nor learned but yet they reside deep within us, there since birth, whether we are aware of their existence or not. Of these instincts, none is more powerful than that of survival. It is a basic characteristic of all living things. People, animals, even plants have survival instincts. When faced with a threat, every ounce of our being shifts into survival mode and we do everything possible to protect ourselves from harm.

Animals live, hunt, and thrive, by their instincts. It may appear that their instinctive nature is stronger than that of the human species because our brains are far more developed and we tend to rely heavily on intellect. We overthink things, we question ourselves, and often we talk ourselves out of following our instincts for one reason or another. I remember a friend who had once found herself in a precarious and potentially dangerous situation telling me that she had resisted her instincts simply because she did not want to be "that person". Men frequently resist their instincts more than women do as our overly developed sense of machismo sometimes gets in the way of good common sense. Heaven forbid we should appear cowardly or unmanly, but truth be told, men fall victim to crime as well. For those reasons, I believe that women are often more safety and security conscious than their testosterone-fueled counterparts.

To better understand our instincts, we must first take a look at where they come from. The human brain is a remarkable computer that is capable of operating at lightning speed, believed to be in the quadrillions of calculations per second. Now, I don't know about you, but I'm having a hard enough time wrapping my head around the idea of a "quadrillion". That is one thousand million million. See what I mean? Apparently, it's a one followed by fifteen zeros, but for our purposes, I'm fine with just calling it a whole heck of a lot.

Our brain is constantly bombarded with data, both internally within our bodies and the external input of everything around us. On a conscious level, we are aware of a countless number of things, but on the sub-conscious level, the number soars. We move through our world totally unaware of the massive amount of data that our brains are collecting and sorting through each and every second. Now there are plenty of theories, but many believe that this is where our sixth sense truly comes from. The product of all of the subliminal stimuli around us processed by the brain in milliseconds resulting in a series of conclusions, whether we are aware of them on a conscious level or not.

The input is taken in by way of our more easily definable five senses; those of sight, sound, taste, touch, and smell. These basic senses are more finely tuned than most people realize and are often greatly underestimated. When we glance down a street, what do we see? We are probably only aware of a handful of things, yet on a subconscious level we see a great deal more. Some of it is right in front of us, but there is much more in our periphery. For that reason, investigators will often use hypnosis as a means to gather information from a witness. In that way, they can access sometimes critical information that the individual did not even realize they had seen or heard.

Some people can utilize one or more of their senses to a greater extent than others, often as a result of a chosen profession or a specific interest. The artist with a keen eye or the musician with a great ear. But do these individuals actually have a superior ability to others? Are they gifted or have they simply developed certain senses to a higher degree? Much like muscles, our senses can be exercised and strengthened. While we all have biceps, most of us will never have arms like Arnold. We can, however, develop what we have and make them stronger.

Personally, I'm not a wine drinker and probably couldn't differentiate between a cheap bottle of red and an expensive Merlot. A Sommelier, on the other hand, an expert in wine, can make precise distinctions in taste and aroma down to the finest detail or notes. Was he born with a magnificent set of taste buds or has he simply developed his sense of taste to a greater degree because of his love of wine?

At this point, you're probably thinking that it must be a monumental task to develop and hone your senses to this level of heightened awareness, and you would be correct. The good news is that you really don't have to. In fact, it's as simple as listening to what your brain is already telling you and trusting those instincts. That feeling in your gut or the little voice whispering in your ear. That is your subconscious mind telling you what it has observed while you didn't think you were paying attention. The stimulus is always there regardless of whether you are consciously taking notice of it or not.

It always amazes me that people are so resistant to following their instincts. How often have we heard someone say "I knew better" or "I had a feeling something was wrong but I ignored it"? We tend to give priority to that which seems logical and discount what we cannot easily rationalize or explain. Time after time, people ignore their instincts out of a sense that they are being paranoid or just plain silly. Sometimes you may have an instinctive feeling that something isn't right or a sense of impending danger and yet nothing bad happens. This, of course, reinforces the notion that such intuition is misguided and foolish but does that necessarily mean that there was no actual threat? The danger may have been very real indeed, but some other factor that you were unaware of changed the circumstances or the outcome.

Soldiers and police officers know from experience to trust those instincts, even when they can't completely understand them at the time. The nature of their jobs puts them at risk and their daily activities can sometimes be fraught with peril. Their survival skills are understandably strong as a result of training, experience, and simply out of necessity. The inherent danger that goes along with their profession puts a target on their backs, so of course, they have a heightened awareness when it comes to their own personal safety. In contrast, most civilians do not often encounter danger and many times don't recognize the warning signs of a threat until it's too late. There are countless stories where a police officer trusted his or her sixth sense to avoid a life-threatening situation but there are plenty of real-world scenarios too. While most people don't face danger on a daily basis as a police officer or combat soldier might, situations sometimes arise during the course of everyday life. Perhaps you have had an experience where your intuition was telling you something that just didn't seem to make sense at the time.

A real estate agent arrives at a house to preview it for a client. The house is vacant and the listing agent told her that the owner had taken a job in another state. She retrieves the key from the lockbox and quickly goes inside. It was the last of four that she had checked out that day and she would only be there for a few minutes before heading over to school in time to get a good spot in the car loop. Making her way from room to room, she begins to feel increasingly uncomfortable. She shakes it off and convinces herself that she is just being silly. After all, she's been alone in countless empty houses before. Maybe it's just because it was kind of a gloomy day outside, or perhaps that episode of Dateline that she watched the night before. She's hurried, distracted, and ignoring her instincts.

So is she just being paranoid or is she disregarding what her sixth sense is telling her? What might her subconscious mind be noticing while she is trying to remember if she faxed that addendum over to the title company this morning? It looks like somebody tracked some dirt in on the carpet... probably just another agent who didn't take the time to wipe their feet. The feeling of the air moving ever so slightly or that the doorknob nearly pulled out of her hand as if a window was open somewhere in the house. What about that faint smell of beer from the six empty cans lying on the bedroom floor? Or perhaps an even more subtle odor, the perspiration of a nervous intruder.

Your subconscious mind will recognize all of the above, but chances are you won't even realize it. You won't be aware of all of the data that your brain is processing on a subconscious level, but your instincts will let you know. Hindsight is 20/20, at least that's what they say, but that excuse doesn't always hold up. How many times have we heard someone claim "well I know that now..." while recounting some unfortunate event? The truth is that they knew it then too, they just didn't accept it as fact at the time. The rational mind is so quick to dismiss our most primal instincts and to ignore those basic survival skills. It can drown out the sound of that little voice whispering in your ear, even when it starts to shout. People love to say "trust your instincts", but in reality, they rarely do. So pay attention to what your sixth sense is trying to tell you. What you do with that information is totally up to you. You can listen to it or ignore it, the choice is yours. I urge you to not only listen to those instincts but to embrace them. If you do, you will experience a heightened sense of awareness that will ultimately help to keep you safe.

"You see but you do not observe."
- Sherlock Holmes

SITUATIONAL AWARENESS   6

"Are you a cop?", she asked with a smile. It's a question that I've been asked countless times throughout my life. It puzzled me for the longest while and I really didn't know what to make of this seemingly odd inquiry. I'd like to think I'm a friendly enough sort and hopefully don't come off as being rigid or unapproachable. I don't have a crew cut and I've worn a beard for most of my adult life, so I really don't think I look the part. I did at one time though, graduating from the Police Academy in southern California way back in 1987. I took a hard left turn into the private sector more than twenty-five years ago but I still get asked that question from time to time.. It used to bother me a little when I was younger, but now I just smile and hope that my eye roll wasn't too obvious.

There was a time that I was very self-conscious about this, and I can remember making a concerted effort not to look so serious and loosen up a bit. After a few years of that, I finally began to respond to this query with one of my own, "Why do you ask?". The answers I would get were as varied as the inquisitors themselves, but I continued to ask and over time, a pattern emerged. While some were rather vague and referred to me as having "cop's eyes", many others were more specific and always referred not just to my eyes but what I was watching. Overall, the general consensus was that I "watch everyone and some people quite intently". While people's efforts to explain what they saw in me often left them searching for the appropriate words, what they were all unknowingly referring to is called "situational awareness".

Some might say that situational awareness is just being highly observant, but observing what is happening around you is only part of the equation. To be truly engaged in the moment, you not only need to observe the environment, events, and people in a given area, you must also interpret the meaning of all of those elements and the relationships that exist between them. If you would describe yourself as observant, then developing a heightened level of situational awareness should not be a difficult task. If, on the other hand, you would more likely be described as "oblivious", then this is going to take a bit more effort on your part. Some people have a natural tendency towards situational awareness and are very cognizant of their surroundings. A perfect, if not ironic example of this are the people who have approached me and asked if I was a cop. Obviously, they had observed my behavior and considered its potential meaning which led them to make certain assumptions.

Now, I'm not going to tell you that I have any kind of superhuman powers, far from it. I'm just a regular person like anyone else. I am, however, incredibly observant and always aware of my surroundings. I notice when a co-worker gets a haircut or changes something about their appearance. To the contrary, I have worked with people who wouldn't notice if someone showed up with their clothes on backwards. As I mentioned, I have always worn a beard and every few years or so I decide to shave it off, a decision that I always seem to regret, as it turns out. What I would always find amusing were the many comments that I'd receive. "Wow, you've really lost some weight", "Is that a new suit?", or "Wow, you've really gained some weight". Some would just squint and wonder what was different. Along that same line, I recently listened to two friends debate whether or not our mutual friend Randy has a mustache. He does, by the way, and I don't think he has ever been without it.

So why do some people see so much while others see so little? It's habit mostly. Some zone out while others zone in, seeing the environment around them in great detail. Simply put, they pay attention to a higher degree than most. That shouldn't be all that hard to do these days considering how many people walk around in a trance-like state, their eyes fixed on their smartphones. On a side note, and speaking of phone-zombies as I like to call them, what would make for a better victim than someone totally oblivious to their surroundings who could be caught completely off guard by a mugger, or worse? Food for thought.

One of the best things about situational awareness is that while it's one of the most effective skills to avoid becoming a victim, it is also one that anyone can master. When learning self-protection, some people may be physically stronger or faster than others and therefore have an advantage. When it comes to being situationally aware, you are relying only on your senses and your ability to pay attention to what you are seeing, hearing, and even smelling. While it is not a difficult skill to master, I am always amazed at how many people travel through life so unaware of what's happening around them.

One example of this occurred while dining out with a friend. It was only recently, but I've seen this same scenario play out countless times in my life, and I would imagine that you have too. Halfway through our meal, my dining companion needed something from the waiter, the same waiter who greeted us, took our order, and brought us our food. Each time a server got near our table, she would ask, "Is that him?". Of course, I was happy to help and call over our waiter. His name was James as I recall, it said so right there on his name tag. This is an obvious example of someone not only being unaware of the people around them but of not even paying attention to someone that they had spoken to just moments before. I'm not trying to be harsh in calling out my friend because unfortunately, this type of inattention has become incredibly common.

Continuing with our dining out scenario, imagine that you and I are sitting in a booth at a local restaurant. If I asked you to close your eyes, what could you tell me about our surroundings? Could you describe our server or the people seated at nearby tables? What color are the walls? If you asked the same of me, I could probably tell you quite a bit. Not only the details mentioned above but also the location of the exits, security cameras, as well as a variety of details about the decor and the other patrons seated nearby. This may seem tedious, but I assure you it is not.

As with any skill, proficiency comes with repetition. Of course, my situational awareness was developed as a direct result of my work experience. When you are responsible for the protection and well-being of others, you are paid to observe people and to view everyone as a potential threat. While in my case, that experience was definitely the catalyst for developing certain skills, anyone can raise the level of their own observational abilities to a point where it becomes second nature. We are constantly surrounded by an inordinate amount of sights and sounds, so much so that they don't even register on a conscious level. That doesn't mean that you haven't seen or heard them. Your sixth sense is always working.

I remember a visit to the grocery store a few years back. As I made my way from aisle to aisle, I found myself thinking about a friend I hadn't heard from in a while and wondered how he was doing. Strangely enough, when I got in line to check out, who do you think was in front of me but my old friend? We chatted for a few minutes and caught up as we walked out to the parking lot with our groceries. It was only then that I realized that his car was parked just two spaces over from mine. I must have walked right past it. It's the same car that he's had for years, same Florida Gators license plate on the back. So was this an incredible coincidence, or what some call the "law of

SITUATIONAL AWARENESS

attraction"? I personally think that I saw his car on the way in without it registering on a conscious level, but if you prefer to subscribe to the mystical thinking outlined in books like "The Secret", by all means, feel free.

So now that we've discussed some examples of situational awareness and the lack thereof, let's focus on how to hone this skill and put it into practice in your everyday life. Begin by making a conscious decision to stop staring at your phone and start paying attention to what is going on around you. Be present in the moment, alert, and observant. It really can be an eye-opening experience, no pun intended. When you walk into a store or restaurant, make a point to look around and take note of what you are seeing. Every moment of your day is filled with countless opportunities to notice your surroundings and the people around you. If you have a friend or co-worker who is willing to play along and improve their own level of attentiveness, you can pose questions to each other to get in the habit of observing. If you have kids, this can be a fun game to keep them occupied and get their noses out of their phones and video games. It will train them from an early age to see what's going on around them, but it will also force you to take notice as well. There are countless ways that you can practice this until it comes naturally. Use your imagination and create exercises that work for you. If you were to only take away one skill from this book, I would hope that it would be an enhanced level of situational awareness. It will help to keep you safe from harm, whether that harm be intentional or accidental, and really can mean the difference between life and death. To illustrate that very point, I will share one last story with you. A story with more serious considerations than haircuts or waiters, and one with potentially greater consequences.

I was traveling cross-country back in the mid-90s. I had gotten a late start on that day, the first of a 2700 mile drive from Southern California back to visit my parents in my home state of New Jersey. I had made my way up the 15 Freeway, through the southern tip of Nevada and well into Utah by late evening, and I was ready to stop for the night. After a long day of driving, I only had three things on my mind - food, hotel, and restroom, not necessarily in that order. I had passed some signs along the way advertising a Holiday Inn and a McDonald's about 25 miles ahead, and that would certainly do just fine. It was around 10 PM when I pulled into the parking lot of Mickey D's and "restroom" had now jumped to the top of my list. I was just south of Provo and definitely far from home.

I'm not sure why, but I parked my car in a spot across the lot from the building, as opposed to a parking space facing in towards the windows. I locked the car and headed for the restaurant. If you remember the layout of McDonald's back then, they were kind of "L" shaped. The front entrance faced the counter where you ordered food and there was a side door at the far end of the L, back where the restrooms were. I crossed the lot and headed for the side door, even though it was a little farther than the front. The place was well lit inside and almost empty. Almost, but not quite. The lone patron, a guy in his mid-twenties I'd say, sat slouched down in his seat in the last booth, back by the restrooms. I noticed him right away, and he definitely seemed to be noticing me. As I got a few steps closer to the building, he abruptly got up and went into the Men's Room. I stopped in my tracks and I'm not kidding when I tell you that the hair stood up on the back of my neck. My thought process was that he saw that I had committed to the side entrance, and one would only take that indirect path if they were headed to the restroom first. I stood there for just a moment and considered my options, silently consulting my common sense and training, not to mention my bladder.

I quickly returned to my car and removed the 9mm pistol from under the driver's seat and tucked it securely in my waistband, just at the small of my back. As I made my way back towards the building, I found myself stopped in the exact same spot as before. I just stood there staring at the brightly lit windows for a moment and asked myself one very important question.... "What the hell are you doing?" Obviously, if I felt threatened enough to feel the need to arm myself before going into a restroom, that was a good enough reason to get back in my car and leave, and that's just what I did.

I would head up the street and find another alternative. I backed my car out of the parking space and can remember feeling foolish, paranoid, and even unmanly to some degree. Perhaps it would have ended up as one of those embarrassing events that I would have kept to myself for all these years, but that's not the case. The reason it didn't, and why I'm still sharing this story all these years later, is because of one other thing that happened as I pulled away. I gave one last glance at the building as I drove out and happened to notice the men's room door slowly opening. Not all the way mind you, just a couple of inches. I also saw a face peeking out as if wondering why I hadn't entered yet.

I don't know what story I would be telling today if I had made different choices that night. Maybe I wouldn't be here to be telling anybody anything. The difference, in my opinion, really came down to situational awareness. Even though I was tired, hungry, and more, I was still alert and aware, and I processed the potential meaning of what I was seeing. Obviously, there is no way of knowing what would have happened for sure, but for me, I have absolutely no doubt in my mind that something bad would have gone down and that I would have been robbed, assaulted, or worse.

I can't tell you how many times I have been asked if it is tiring to look at everyone and everything with such a critical eye. In reality, there is a tremendous difference between being suspicious and being aware, and I can assure you that the latter is not at all tedious. With a little patience, it will in time become second nature. Your mind has the ability to process a tremendous amount of information, and it can sort and categorize all of that data on a subconscious level. In a world filled with increasing distraction, exercising situational awareness and simply practicing the lost art of paying attention will serve you well.

ON THE ROAD AGAIN 7

If you're like most real estate agents that I know, you probably spend as much time behind the wheel of your car as you do at your desk. It's far more than a way to get from point A to point B and can sometimes feel like your second office. Just like every other tool of your trade, your vehicle is an integral part of your job, and as a vital part of your daily activities, it is one that you are rarely without. Most agents know that a newer model car presents a successful image to potential clients, but as an asset, it can also garner the attention of the criminal element. After all, it is more than likely the most valuable item that you have with you at any given time. Beyond serving as a mobile office and a mode of transportation, in a dangerous situation, your vehicle can serve as a lockable safe room, a method of escape, and even as a weapon. In the most dire of circumstances, it can also become a crime scene.

The most common form of auto-related crime is the theft of property from inside of a vehicle. Your purse, laptop, tablet, and smartphone are all valuable items that we often leave clearly visible on the front seats of our cars. The first and most obvious theft deterrent is to simply lock your vehicle. I am constantly amazed at how many people will leave their vehicles unlocked overnight in their driveways. It is a low-risk crime for a couple of teenagers to make their way up the street trying door handles until they find an open one. It's not uncommon for several cars to be burglarized in one neighborhood on the same night, and there is little chance of being noticed at 3 AM. It's what law enforcement refers to as a "crime of opportunity", and it is up to you to eliminate that opportunity. I'm always shocked to hear of computers, checkbooks, and even firearms being stolen from vehicles left unlocked overnight. The trunk may seem like a more secure location but since most automobiles have trunk releases, this is only effective if the car is locked.

Now that we have taken the incredibly high-tech countermeasure of locking the vehicle, it's also important to remember to keep valuables concealed and out of plain sight. A criminal will be much more likely to risk breaking and entering a car if he can see what his ultimate payoff will be, as opposed to burglarizing a vehicle in hopes that there might be something of value inside. Secure your property in the trunk or glove compartment to avoid enticing any would-be thieves.

Recently, there has been a new type of theft taking place known as "sliding", and it occurs while the unsuspecting victim is getting gas. While you are dispensing fuel at the rear of the car, the thief approaches from the passenger side of the vehicle staying low and out of sight. He quickly and quietly opens the car door and removes whatever valuables are on the passenger seat. Sliding is a crime usually perpetrated against women and the most common items stolen are purses as men are more likely to keep their wallet in a pants or coat pocket. If you think that you are much too aware to ever be a victim of this type of theft, take a look online and watch some security camera footage of these crooks in action and how smoothly they can perpetrate this crime. By the time you have finished gassing up and get back into your car, the thief is long gone.

Beyond theft of property from a vehicle, there is, of course, the risk of the car itself being stolen. In the old days, car thieves targeted unattended vehicles armed only with a modest amount of gumption and a Slim Jim. The unsuspecting owner of the car only discovered some time later that they had been the victim of a crime, often left to scratch their heads in the middle of a parking lot saying "I could've sworn I parked here...". Unfortunately, criminals of all types have become increasingly brazen and the car thief is no different. While it is a more confrontational crime with the associated possibility of violence, carjacking is certainly a more efficient crime from the criminal's standpoint. No need to break and enter or to go to the trouble of hot-wiring the ignition when the vehicle is unlocked and already running.

While some carjackers will simply order you out of your vehicle at gunpoint when you are stopped at a traffic light, there is more often than not some sort of ploy to get you to pull over and stop your car. As with any type of crime prevention, it is important to know what approach a criminal might take so that you can recognize it when it occurs and hopefully avoid being victimized. Below are a few of the most common tactics that a carjacker will employ and methods that you can use to combat them.

The Bump

The carjacker will hit the target vehicle from behind. The unsuspecting victim will pull over to assess the damage and exchange information, at which time the vehicle will be taken. There will almost always be two perpetrators of this crime, one to drive the stolen vehicle and one to drive the suspect vehicle. The thieves will have been following the target car for a little while. They can carry out their plan at any point but will seek to do so when you are in a less crowded area. If this should happen, you must resist the urge to immediately pull over and get out of your car. They are counting on you to react emotionally and do exactly that, fueled by your annoyance that someone just hit your car. Turn on your emergency flashers and signal for the other driver to follow you to the nearest busy and well-lit location. The parking lot of just about any type of store that is open for business will fit the bill. Criminals don't like retail parking lots as most of them have active security cameras these days. Additionally, don't park in the far reaches of the lot but as close to the store as possible. If there are no spaces available you can stop in the fire zone along the curb. The attention of the police or a security officer would not be unwelcome. Another approach would be to call 911 and advise the dispatcher that you have been involved in a minor traffic accident and that you are alone and uncomfortable getting out of the car.

The Good Samaritan

In this scenario, the criminals will stage some sort of accident or injury, relying on your kindness and willingness to stop and assist. Most people won't stop for someone simply flagging them down, but will eagerly do so if there seems to be some kind of emergency. Unless you are a trained medical professional or have some other sort of relevant background, the best way you are able to help is to lock your doors and immediately call 911. If the individuals asking you to stop are up to no good, they won't stick around for too long if they see you are on the phone. Give the dispatcher any pertinent information including license plate numbers and descriptions.

The Ruse

This approach involves the carjacker falsely advising you that there is a problem with your car. They may pull alongside you and signal for you to roll down your window alerting you that you have a flat tire or some other mechanical issue. The response to this type of ploy is the same as it is for The Bump, as they will try to get you to pull over at a location of their choosing. Drive to a safe place that is well lit and crowded where you feel safe to exit your vehicle and assess the situation.

The Litter Ploy

The thief will target a desirable car or cars in a crowded parking lot and place some sort of flier, note, or debris, on one of the windows. He won't place it on the driver's side of the windshield but rather the passenger side or often on the rear window. I have even heard of instances where a photocopy of a twenty dollar bill was slipped under the passenger side windshield wiper. The victim enters the car and starts the engine, only to notice the item on the windshield or that their view to back out is obstructed. The unsuspecting driver exits the vehicle to retrieve whatever was left on the car, leaving the door open and the engine running, only to have our patiently waiting car thief slip behind the wheel to make his getaway. It's actually a pretty clever scheme. If only these criminal types would use their ingenuity towards something more noble.

The methods above are the most common used by criminals, but the list is certainly not all-inclusive. Thieves are constantly coming up with new and creative ways to deceive their victims, so use your common sense. If something doesn't seem right, listen to your instincts. A person who means you no harm won't be offended by the fact that you are being cautious. It's important to keep in mind that once the opportunity for avoidance has passed, the next best outcome for the criminal is escape. Your vehicle is his mechanism for doing so. If a criminal is poised to take your car and leave the scene, you should absolutely let him do so. No vehicle is worth risking your life to protect.

The most serious threat to consider when discussing any type of vehicle safety is your passenger. For it is he who poses the most ominous threat to your well-being. You should pre-qualify every prospect prior to going anywhere with them and their information should be on file at your office, not just on your cellphone or in your purse. There is absolutely no excuse for having a total stranger in the car with you. It is as reckless as picking up a random hitchhiker. A predator will always desire a sheltered place to perpetrate his crime, one where he is alone with his victim with little chance of interference from a good Samaritan. Your car certainly fits the bill. It is private, somewhat soundproof, and can be obscured even further if you happen to have tinted windows. It can also serve as a criminal's mode of escape or to transport his victim to a secondary crime scene. In future chapters, we will discuss in more detail the importance of avoiding being taken to a secondary crime scene as your chances of survival diminish greatly under those circumstances. It is always preferable to fight for your life than to be taken to a secluded place where there is little hope of escape.

As a rule of thumb, you should always be the driver when traveling with a prospect. Maintaining control of a given situation is imperative and is the most crucial aspect of safety and security. A criminal will always try to control his victim just as a police officer will take control of a suspect. When you become a passenger, you surrender a great deal of that control, even if it just means the ability to leave at your choosing should your potential client begin to make you feel uncomfortable. A predator has less ability to force you to do something if you are the driver of the car. He may have a weapon and may threaten to use it if you do not obey his commands, but he will be risking his own life if he were to harm you while you are behind the wheel of a moving automobile. For that reason, you are safer in a moving vehicle than in a stationary one. If the car is moving, keep moving. If it is parked, put it in gear and start driving. If you hit traffic, drive on the shoulder. If you encounter a red light, make a right turn on red. Anything to keep moving. Obviously, being pulled over for a traffic violation would be just fine at this point. If you see a police car on the road, do something to get the officer's attention like driving erratically or running a stop sign. Once a vehicle is stopped it is just like any other crime scene and the predator is in control. By controlling a moving automobile, you are by extension, retaining control of the situation.

A criminal who confronts you in a vehicle will inevitably tell you where he wants you to go. He will be directing you to an isolated location, to a secondary crime scene. Obviously, this is a terrifying situation to be in, but you must know going in that the danger only increases if you follow his instructions. His objective is to take you somewhere secluded, but you must remain where there are people. If you are not in a busy area, drive to one. Go to the most crowded place that you know of. A busy supermarket parking lot or crowded shopping center. Police stations and fire stations are also excellent places to get the help that you need.

Once you have taken the steps to drive to a place that is to your advantage and not the predator's, he will be forced to take action in order to regain control. Your intent at this point must be to limit his alternatives, to narrow his choices down to only two - flee or be captured. Your objective should first be to eliminate the car as a means of escape. In simplest terms, you must render the vehicle useless to him. If he is forced to flee on foot, he will leave you behind. You can do this by throwing the keys out the window if possible, or of course, you could take more drastic measures. Crashing the car in a crowded location may sound extreme, but considering this scenario, it is definitely the lesser of two evils. Be sure to avoid bystanders and seek out a target that will sufficiently damage the car like a light pole or other fixed structure that is anchored to the ground and will not budge. Strike the object with the passenger side of the vehicle in hopes that your assailant will take the brunt of the impact. Additionally, damaging the front wheel and/or wheel well area will hopefully render the vehicle undrivable. You will want to be traveling fast enough to disable the car but not so fast as to risk serious injury to yourself. Impacting a fixed structure at 30-35 miles an hour will do a considerable amount of damage to the vehicle and if you are wearing a seatbelt and your car is equipped with airbags, hopefully, you will not be seriously injured. I know that may not sound encouraging, but we are talking about dire circumstances here.

After the vehicle has come to a stop, you will likely attract the attention of anyone in the area. Remember, to the typical bystander, you have only been involved in a traffic accident. You must do everything in your power to attract as much attention as possible and to make it apparent that you are the victim of a crime. If you can get out of the car, do so, and run towards people. Yell, scream and do whatever is necessary to make sure they know what is happening. If you can't get out of the car. Lean on the horn. Tell everyone within earshot, "Help, I am being kidnapped!".

In this chapter, we have run through several scenarios that have forced you to contemplate things that you probably would rather ignore. If there is one common theme throughout this book, it is to provoke thought and encourage you to consider these scenarios so that you will have a plan of action in mind if you are ever confronted by a criminal. If the worst should happen, you will not have the time nor the clarity to assess the situation and figure out what to do. Forethought and preparation are the best tools to ensure your survival.

Now, I would like to think that this last paragraph goes without saying, but I'm going to say it anyway. While the idea of a predator in your car is frightening enough, there is someone else who can pose an even greater threat. Spending so much time in your vehicle often means that you will be multi-tasking, and that is understandable. Time behind the wheel can serve double duty as an opportunity to check messages, return phone calls, and to schedule showings. If your car is not equipped with Bluetooth, hands-free units can be purchased very inexpensively. There are more deaths each year attributed to inattentive driving than by all other vehicle-related causes combined. Keep in mind that while you may be driving responsibly, others on the road might not be. Stay alert, drive defensively, and above all else, please, PLEASE, never text and drive.

VEHICLE SAFETY CHECKLIST

Keep valuables secured in a locked trunk - There is no sense leaving valuables in plain sight to entice any morally sub-standard passers-by.

Keep your doors locked - While driving, parked, or gassing up. If so equipped, program your car's remote to only open the driver's door. It can be set to open the other doors by pressing the button a second time.

Park in well lit, crowded locations - People and lights are a criminal's enemy. Use both to your advantage.

Don't box yourself in - While driving in traffic or stopped at a traffic light, always leave space between you and the car in front of you. This offers you a means of escape in the event of a carjacking attempt.

Avoid high crime areas - Obviously, some neighborhoods are worse than others and risks escalate after dark. Do your best to avoid them. If your destination is in a bad area, take someone with you. If you will merely be passing through a high crime area, consider another route. It will be worth the extra few minutes to keep you safe.

Keep your vehicle gassed up - Your car is your primary method of escape in a crisis so keep it ready to go. Additionally, fueling your vehicle before it is on "E" will avoid having to stop for gas in a bad area or at a less desirable time of day.

Take a picture of your license plate with your phone - What is your license plate number? Do you know? Many people don't. Tag numbers change and it can be even more difficult to recall under the stress of just having been victimized.

Don't stop for strangers - This may seem uncaring but everyone has a cell phone these days. Call 911 to dispatch police, fire, or medical assistance if you feel it is warranted, or even if you are not sure what the problem is. Remember, a criminal will always rely on your kindness.

OPEN HOUSE 8

One of the more routine activities that may expose a real estate agent to risk is that of holding an open house. While this is an excellent way to showcase a property and hopefully secure a contract, there are many inherent risks involved with such an event. When dealing with clients, you have ample opportunity to screen and pre-qualify them, whereas in the case of an open house, you literally never know who might walk in the door. Many articles offering "tips" on conducting safe open houses will suggest using a sign in sheet at the front door. I have mentioned it before and will mention it again, try to think like a criminal and not like a victim. If a predator is there to rob or harm you, he certainly will not hesitate to lie about his identity.

As with many of the security measures outlined in this book, preparation and forethought will go a long way towards minimizing risk. Often, an agent will resist taking steps to ensure their safety, citing concerns that they will hamper sales, but I could not disagree more. Safety and productivity do not have to compete with one another. In fact, many of the precautions outlined below will actually increase foot traffic and visibility, and help to ensure the success of your open house.

By far, the most effective way to safeguard your event is to deprive a potential predator of the "one on one" time that he requires to successfully commit a crime. The simplest way to accomplish this is to generate foot traffic. A constant flow of visitors will keep your open house bustling and that is obviously good for business as well. Advertising, fliers, balloons, and lawn signs, as well as signs around the neighborhood directing traffic in your direction, will go a long way towards drawing people to your event. Of course, all of this should come as no surprise to you and should be an integral part of your marketing plan, but as you also know, not all houses draw as many prospects as you would like. It's important to keep in mind that not everyone visiting an open house needs to be a serious buyer. Neighbors can be a tremendous source of foot traffic as most will be curious and interested in comparing the house with their own in an effort to estimate their property's value. While plenty of neighbors will be interested in taking a peak, many will stay away simply because they do not want to appear nosey. Be sure to tell your homeowner to let the neighbors know about the open house and invite them to stop by. You can obviously do the same by dropping off fliers to neighboring houses to make sure that they know that they are more than welcome. Each of these people that you may dismiss as a looky-loo is good for safety purposes, but with a little politeness, may end up being a prospect at some point down the road. I also believe that a busy open house makes the home appear as a "hot property" as opposed to the one with seemingly little interest.

Beyond all of these effective marketing methods, let's face it, there are some properties that just don't generate much interest. The neighborhood, housing market, price point as well as the general appearance and condition of the house are all part of the equation. Even if you do create an ample amount of foot traffic, there will still be down times that you will be on your own. The buddy system works great to eliminate time alone at the property. A second agent can be very helpful at a busy open house, especially now that your efforts have hopefully generated prospects. A fellow agent/friend could be there to help out with the event, and you, in turn, could do the same for him or her.

Rookie agents can also be an option if you are striking out with your usual list of "buddies". It can be a valuable learning experience for a new licensee, and they should be eager to take you up on the offer. Other resources from within your own group of professional contacts include mortgage reps or brokers that you have worked with in the past. They may be willing to join you at an open house simply for the opportunity to give out business cards and literature to drum up some business of their own. If all else fails, a friend or family member can keep you company if you do not have an associate available to assist you.

Now that we've done our best to minimize, if not eliminate, time alone at the open house, let's move on to some simple and practical steps that you can take to keep yourself safe during the event. When you arrive at the home, be sure to park your car where you cannot be blocked in, preferably on the street. Remember, your car is your means of escape if a problem should arise. For the same reason, your keys should be with you at all times and not left somewhere in the house. Beyond having them on your person if you should have to leave suddenly, your car may be stolen if a visitor happens across your car keys. Your purse should be secured in the trunk of your locked vehicle and not brought inside. An agent once told me that she is always very careful to tuck away her purse and keys somewhere out of sight in the house, as if people at an open house won't open drawers or closets.

If you are like most real estate agents, the first thing you will do upon arrival is to do a walk-through of the house. You'll check every room with a keen eye, taking notice of minor details that others might miss, and do any last minute tidying up that may be necessary. This is an important step to ensure that the house is presentable and "show ready", but it also gives you a chance to view the house from a safety standpoint. First and foremost, you should ensure that the house is indeed empty and that there are no signs of forced entry. This is especially true of vacant homes, and a serious concern with houses that have been empty for an extended period. Over time, it becomes apparent that a house is vacant, especially to those looking for such opportunities. Newspapers on the driveway or an unkempt yard are a good indication of an empty house. Delinquent teens looking to vandalize or party and the homeless looking for a place to bed down for the night have all been known to break and enter vacant houses. The last thing you want to do is find some miscreant sleeping it off on the floor in the back bedroom. Check the house thoroughly and carefully, not only for people but for signs that someone has been there.

You should also familiarize yourself with the floor plan and have an understanding of potential escape routes. Know where all exits are located and be sure that they are unlocked. Check the backyard as well. Is it open or fenced? If fenced, are there gates, and if so, are they locked? If it is a large piece of property, know where the nearest neighbors are. Take notice of interior doors that lock from the opposite side as this is potentially somewhere that you can be locked in to. A door leading to the basement or attic is a prime example of this. People will often install a lock on those doors for added security if someone should break in from either of those locations. It's also very common to see a deadbolt mounted high on a basement door and out of reach of young children, protecting them from taking a tumble down the stairs.

An additional amenity of the house that should catch your eye is the alarm system, if the house is so equipped. A keypad near the entry door is your first clue, and if it is currently being used, the owners may have even given you an access code. If the alarm is functional, it will probably have one or more panic buttons. Most keypads will have one and there may be additional buttons throughout the house. They may be in a fixed location or portable, much like your car's remote. This information can usually be obtained from the owner in advance of the open house. If it is a monitored alarm, the panic button will contact the police, but even an unmonitored system should trigger a siren. The alarm may also have a door chime feature that will sound when a door is opened, alerting you to visitors. I know one clever agent who would bring a bell designed to hang over the top of the door and serve the same purpose, much like an old-time general store.

While taking your first walk-through, you should also keep an eye out for any valuable items left out by the homeowners and take steps to safeguard them. These include items such as cash, jewelry, weapons, prescription medications, and other various valuables or collectibles that are small enough to be stolen and concealed by a thief. While these items have obvious monetary value, there are other items in the house that are often overlooked by the owners. We live in an age where our personal information can have more value than any tangible trinkets. Identity theft is becoming incredibly common and it doesn't take much to unlock a wealth of information to those who are so inclined. An unsecured laptop, a bank statement, or a stack of unopened mail, are all potential sources of sensitive information. I'm sure you can see the danger here, but it's not only financial data that we must protect. If I walked through your home right now, what could I learn about you and your loved ones? While most people will remember to clear off their desk of any important papers, it's often the refrigerator that gives the most insight into people's lives. The activities and schedules of not only yourself but of your children are right there in plain sight. The open house may pass without incident, but a forward-thinking criminal may be back after checking out the house and noticing the big calendar on your kitchen wall. Sure, that picture of the two Siamese kittens is adorable, but he's more interested in the fact that you will be going to visit Grandma for ten days next month.

Well, you're just about ready to open the doors and get that house sold. If you include the methods outlined above when planning and holding your next open house, you will have done a great deal to ensure that your event will be a successful and safe one. In the following chapter, we will discuss ways to safeguard yourself while showing a property that can be used whether you are holding an open house or during a typical showing.

OPEN HOUSE CHECKLIST

Park where you will not be blocked in – Preferably on the street and not in the driveway. Your purse and other valuables should be locked in the trunk.

Bring a "buddy" - A fellow agent, mortgage broker, friend, or family member can ensure that you will not be alone during the open house.

Do a thorough walkthrough – Before the event begins. Check that the house is truly empty and that the owners have not left anything of value lying around. Take note of points of exit that would serve as an escape route.

Keep your keys and phone with you – 911 and other emergency contacts should be pre-programmed.

Don't turn your back – Let the visitor take the lead and direct them verbally. Avoid dead-end spaces and lockable areas where you can be boxed in.

Thoroughly check the house – Make sure that everyone who entered has actually left. Double-check all windows and doors to make sure they are locked. Leave WITH your buddy. "I'll be right behind you." is unacceptable.

SHOW AND TELL   9

If you look at the statistics, real estate agents are most often victimized while showing property. For this reason, predators will commonly portray themselves as home buyers in an effort to create the opportunity to perpetrate their crime. As I have mentioned countless times before, privacy is an absolute necessity for a criminal to be successful as his primary objective is to get you alone in an isolated location. Your first line of defense is to try to deprive him of this by bringing a colleague or friend along with you, but we both know that is not always practical. So let's move on to the steps you can take to stay safe while showing an empty property to a prospect.

While this may be redundant, let's go over some of the basic safety measures that you should take before the actual showing. First and foremost, always avoid meeting a stranger for the first time at a property. A client should be properly pre-screened, and their identifying information should be recorded at the office prior to any showings. Potential buyers will often call on a property that they have seen and request a showing. While this is certainly common practice in the realty business and most prospects are exactly what they portray themselves to be, it's almost always the tactic that a predator will try to employ. You can ask the buyer to meet you at the office first and then proceed to the property from there. If they are too insistent, this might be a red flag. As inadvisable as it may be, sometimes you may be have to meet a buyer for the first time at a property. If that is the case, by all means, take someone with you. As the old saying goes, there's safety in numbers.

While honesty and integrity should always be the most important considerations when conducting business, I am of the opinion that using the occasional ruse for the sole purpose of personal safety is perfectly acceptable. When speaking to a potential buyer on the phone, you may choose to use the terms "we" and "us" instead of "I", implying that you will not be coming alone. Also, you should avoid describing the property as "vacant" and can always make reference to the owners or current occupants in conversation.

"I will check with the owners to make sure that will be a convenient time."

While showing a home, you can also mention that another agent is bringing buyers to the property shortly. Your phone can be used for a number of ploys by calling a friend while with the client.

"Jill, can you bring that paperwork by? I'm at 123 First Street with Mr. Smith."

Making a potential criminal aware that you are in constant contact with your office and associates will go a long way towards discouraging him. Use your imagination. There are many ways that you can create the impression that someone is on the way to your location at that very moment.

Criminals like the nighttime for a reason. There are fewer people out and about in the evening and darkness can conceal a great deal, like a physical description or a license plate number. You should always limit your showings to daytime hours. For you commercial real estate agents out there, you need to be especially aware as commercial properties offer their own distinct challenges and can become extremely desolate after 4 PM and on weekends and holidays.

When you arrive at the property, be sure to park where you can not be blocked in, preferably on the street. At this point, you should be alert and aware. Take a moment to observe your surroundings. Once inside the property, it's easy for you to focus your attention on the house itself, especially if you haven't been there before. It is important to remain attentive to the client and observe his or her actions as they will provide telltale signs if they have something other than house hunting in mind. If their intent is to simply look at a property, they will do just that. Be wary of a client who does not seem too interested in the house or seems to be looking out the windows a little too much. While your client should be totally focused on the amenities of the house, you have the perfect opportunity to observe them and look for any signs of nervousness or unusual body language.

As you move through the house, you should keep your car keys with you and accessible. Aside from the obvious ease of escape, there are other reasons to keep them with you at all times. The remote for your car is one of the most simple, effective, and overlooked, safety devices available to just about anyone. Most modern key fobs have a panic button on them. It's a feature that is always forgotten until you accidentally hit it while unloading groceries from your car. While some of you may be conscious of its existence, most people limit their view of the panic button's usefulness to mall parking lots and deserted parking garages. Your car's remote usually has a fairly decent range, and can often be triggered from inside the house. Now, I don't know about you, but I doubt a criminal would stick around for too long while an alarm was blaring from the car parked on the street in front of the house. By the way, this can also be a great security device in your own home. Leaving your car keys on your bedside table gives you quick access to a panic button. Test this out and see if it will set off the car's alarm while it's parked in your garage or driveway.

While it seems that actual car keys are becoming less and less common, most people carry a host of other keys on their key ring, and they can be an excellent improvised weapon if needed. Clutch your key ring in your fist with two or three keys sticking out from between your fingers and your hand has just become a much more formidable weapon. Also carried on your person at all times should be your cell phone and any weapons that you may choose to carry. I highly recommend pepper spray for defensive purposes. Be sure to read the chapter on that topic if you have any doubts as to its effectiveness as a weapon.

As you take the buyer on a tour of the house, it is important to maintain control, not only of the situation but of the client as well. Let them lead the way as you move from room to room. You can verbally direct them and point out the home's features. When you show bedrooms or other dead-end spaces, remain at the doorway letting your client move about the room while still able to converse with you. From a sales standpoint, this will also tend to make the room seem bigger as it will be less crowded. By allowing the other party to take the lead and mentally take ownership of the house, you also ensure that you will not be turning your back on them. The objective should be to keep the prospect in sight at all times. An assailant will usually prefer to attack someone when they are at their most vulnerable, very often from behind. As mentioned previously in the chapter pertaining to open houses, be aware of areas of the house with locking doors, like basement and attic stairways.

As a salesperson, it is always advisable to be warm and friendly as one of your primary goals is to establish a rapport with your client. Of course, this is absolutely appropriate behavior, but be careful not to divulge too much personal information about yourself. While our focus in this chapter is to avoid being attacked while showing property, it is important to keep in mind the possibility of being victimized by that individual at some point down the road. Your buyer may become fixated or obsessed with you, exposing you to the threat of stalking or a future assault. Be friendly, but always keep it professional.

Beyond the first priority of personal safety, your secondary concern should be that of protecting the property itself and the interests of the owners. Your client may have no intention of harming you but may have sticky fingers when it comes to valuables left around the house. Obviously, this is another reason to keep your prospect in sight at all times. There are plenty of people out there who don't set out to steal but may not resist the urge if the opportunity presents itself. Once you show the property, you also have an extended responsibility for the physical security of the house itself. It is not uncommon for a thief to view a home with the intention of casing the property and leaving a back door or window unlocked, allowing easy access when they return at a future time. As a matter of professionalism, you should always leave a property exactly as you found it and be sure that all windows are locked and doors are deadbolted. Keys should be returned to the appropriate lockbox and properly secured.

INFORMATION SECURITY   10

What is your most valuable asset? If you asked ten people this question, you would more than likely get ten completely different answers. Just as beauty is in the eye of the beholder, value is an equally subjective concept. What is considered precious and cherished by one, may be of little or no worth to another. As they say, "One man's trash is another man's treasure". Of the variety of responses that you would likely receive to such an inquiry, the answers would range from items that have a monetary worth to those possessions with value that is far more difficult to measure. Some may speak of houses and automobiles, or possibly stock portfolios and jewelry. For others, their prized possessions may be ones that hold sentimental value such as a family heirloom. Considering the fact that an asset need only be possessed but not necessarily owned, some might answer in a far more abstract way, citing the value of family and friends or perhaps their own honor and integrity.

Obviously, all of these assets would hold great value to each of these people, and we could debate endlessly as to which is the more valuable, but we would be remiss if we did not include another asset on this list. Often overlooked is one's own identity, the personal data that makes you who you are, at least on paper. Its worth may be abstract, but in the wrong hands, it can devalue each of the items listed above. Of course, financially valuable assets may be compromised, but your honesty and character could also be called into question and even irreparably damaged, not to mention your creditworthiness. Like all other assets, your personal information, financial or otherwise, must be properly safeguarded and secured.

In years past, this was much easier to accomplish than in today's world where information and money are sent electronically and business is routinely conducted in cyberspace. There was a time when tearing up the carbon copy of your credit card slip was the extent of your informational security measures. While credit card slips are a thing of the past, some basic measures from the old days

INFORMATION SECURITY

are still considered wise precautions. Shredding documents and blacking out sensitive information is always a good idea, and physically safeguarding paperwork is still as important as it ever was.

As a real estate agent, you should be well aware that protecting personal information from financial fraud and identity theft not only applies to your own data but also to the sensitive information of each person that you deal with. In fact, when it comes to your clients, it is a matter of law. In a fiduciary relationship, it is the duty of the real estate agent or broker to protect the client's privacy and keep all information confidential unless required to divulge it by a court of law. Many agents leave a tremendous amount of paperwork littered on their desks, swearing that they have their own filing system and know exactly where everything is. Well, I don't want to be the neatness police, but amongst that clutter of paperwork is bound to be identifying information regarding at least one of your clients. When I ask some agents about that, they assure me that only other agents and staff have access to the back office and that there is absolutely nothing to worry about. They usually don't have quite as quick of a response when I ask them what company cleans their office at night and who maintains the building. It's not elves who are changing the light bulbs and emptying the wastebaskets at night, long after you've left for the evening.

Since much of your business is conducted in the virtual world, it goes to reason that most information crime also takes place in cyberspace. The internet and smartphone technology have arguably been the greatest advances to commerce in our lifetime, and the real estate business is no exception. Unless you are a dinosaur, you use these tools countless times per day in the course of your daily activities for both business purposes and personal. Along with this added convenience comes added risk. Credit card information, social security numbers, account numbers, drivers license numbers, home addresses, and dates of birth are all very valuable pieces of information to the cyber-criminal or predator.

Like most people, you probably take some precautions when using your laptop or cell phone, but identity theft has become rampant and if you don't take this matter seriously, it's just a matter of time before your information, or that of your client, is compromised. You should, of course, be using an anti-virus program. Most computers come with some type of security software pre-installed these days. You should keep it set to run regular virus scans and also to be actively monitoring your computer for incoming threats. When it comes to software, there are numerous options available, some for a price and many others for free. For the sake of redundancy, I keep two programs installed and running on my laptop at all times and scan with both on a regular basis. As with all software, it is important to keep your computer's security measures up to date. The miscreants who create the various types of malware and viruses are always coming up with something new, and in turn, the anti-virus folks are consistently updating definitions and devising countermeasures. Your computer security software is only effective if it is up to date, and you should have it set to update automatically on a weekly basis.

Due to the expansive amount of personal information contained on your computer, it is important to physically safeguard it, just as you would keep a safe locked or a filing cabinet secured. The machine itself should be password protected, as should any other devices such as a tablet or cell phone, and the password should be something impossible to guess. Avoid using birthdays, children's names, and any other words that would be easy for a cyber-criminal to figure out. Change your passwords on a regular basis as even the best passwords can be compromised. You should also be very cautious regarding any device that you physically connect to your computer by way of a USB port or wirelessly via Bluetooth. Just like a flu bug, computer viruses are highly contagious and are intentionally designed to spread from one machine to another.

Continuing on the topic of the physical security of your computer, here is a rather unsettling threat that you may not be aware of. If you have ever used Skype or any other type of video chat platform, you know that your laptop is equipped with a webcam. Some years back this was a clunky add-on that clipped onto your computer, but now it is a built-in part of most machines. If you are not familiar with it, it's that little dot above your laptop screen. Once a cyber-criminal has hacked into your computer, he can access just about any program, including the webcam, allowing him to remotely watch whatever the webcam is seeing. This can be done even if you are not using your computer, while it's sitting idle on your desk or coffee table. Very creepy, I know, but there is a very simple solution to this. Just apply a band-aid or a piece of electrical tape over the camera lens when not in use. I'm not sure how rampant this type of cyber-peeping is, but this low-tech countermeasure will provide you with considerable peace of mind.

Beyond the dangers mentioned above, your computer and cell phone are also at risk via the various wi-fi networks that they connect to, whether you are aware of the connection or not. If you keep your device set to automatically connect to available networks, you are asking for trouble. It is important to approve all wi-fi connections for obvious reasons, but it also serves as a reminder that you are connecting to a public network. That college kid slumped in his chair at Starbucks might not be studying for exams but rather trolling the public network and trying to access the devices of other patrons who only wanted to feed their caffeine addiction and check out what's new on Facebook. Hackers have also been known to set up their own public wi-fi, often in crowded urban areas, for no other reason than to compromise the information of anyone who comes into range and unwittingly connects to the network.

Computers have obviously made our lives far more convenient and replaced the way that we perform many of our daily tasks. Of all of these innovations, none has had more of an impact than the advent of email. The days of correspondence via the United States Postal Service are rapidly becoming a thing of the past. I honestly can't recall the last time I bought stamps and my mailbox usually contains nothing more than annoying advertisements, although I do miss the occasional letter from Ed McMahon advising that I may "Already be a Winner!" While email is a convenient and instantaneous way to correspond, it also poses new dangers that we must be on the lookout for. In the old days, a chain letter was pretty easy to recognize as shady, but today's online hooligans are far more creative. Sure, the emails from the Nigerian Prince or the Ukrainian Lottery are easy to spot, but some others are very difficult to discern from the real thing. I consistently receive emails, allegedly from my bank, the IRS, and the FBI, among others, all fraudulent of course. While these emails may look legitimate, they will usually prompt the reader to follow a link or dial a number where someone will try to obtain information from you. If you are unsure of the authenticity of one of these emails, contact the bank or company in question via a phone number or web address that you know to be correct.

Aside from the most blatant scams, even legitimate email correspondence can be a target for the identity thief and other cyber-criminals. While you may take every precaution with your computer and the sensitive information that it contains, you cannot be sure of the diligence of the email's recipient. If you include sensitive information in an email or attached files, that information is now in a folder somewhere on another person's computer and susceptible to the same threats that you have taken steps to guard against. Avoid sending personal information by email if possible and blackout specific areas containing sensitive information before scanning.

While many criminals have come up with an array of high tech schemes to attempt to defraud you, many others still use the old tried and true methods that have unfortunately worked for decades. The elderly are often targeted by phone, but some of the ruses sound incredibly convincing and just about any unsuspecting person can fall victim. Much like the bogus email approach, many of these scammers will leave a message on the victims answering machine, alerting them of an alleged problem and ask that they call to straighten it out. Sometimes the objective will be to get the subject to divulge personal information, but other times the phone call itself can be the culprit. For example, you receive a message stating some discrepancy on a bank account or that there may have been fraudulent charges on your credit card. Of course, you are concerned and dial the number that was left. It all seems legit because the person on the other end of the phone is not asking for any sensitive information. They will often transfer your call or put you on hold, but this becomes endless as the only objective is to keep you on the phone for as long as possible. You finally hang up and call the number on your statement to find out that there was no problem at all. Everything seems fine until you receive your phone bill and discover that the number you dialed was to a pay per call number, similar to the old 900 and 976 exchanges. Sometimes these numbers may be located outside the country, and well out of reach of the FCC. Years ago, in the days of dial-up internet, my computer contracted a virus that disconnected me from the internet and then had my computer dial one of these numbers. Unbeknownst to me, I was connected to the Island nation of Vanuatu and the meter was definitely running.

You should keep in mind that this chapter is only the tip of the iceberg when it comes to information and cyber-security. A great many books have been written on the subject and often become obsolete within months as the criminals continue to come up with new and improved ways to swindle the public at large. Generally speaking, be protective of all of your information and that of your clients. Think of it as you would cash. It is just as valuable and you certainly wouldn't leave it lying around or unsecured. Identity theft and cyber-crime are the fastest growing segments of criminal enterprise, and there is no reason to believe that this trend will not continue.

BY THE NUMBERS

16.7 MILLION people were impacted by identity theft in 2017 alone totaling **16.8 BILLION DOLLARS** stolen. - Javelin Strategy & Research

Email fraud remains the **#1 CYBERCRIME**. - Federal Bureau of Investigation

Cybercrime will cost businesses over **2 TRILLION DOLLARS** by the year 2019. - Juniper Research

46% of American Consumers have had their credit card information compromised in the last 5 years. - ACI Worldwide

It is expected that **146 BILLION** data records will be stolen by the year 2023 - Juniper Research

"Technology alone is not enough"
- Steve Jobs

TECH TALK   11

Unless you've been living in a cave for the last several years, I'm sure you have noticed the many ways that technology has become an integral part of our everyday lives. Imagine if we could go back in time twenty years and glimpse into the future to see what today's world would be like. We probably would have thought we stumbled onto a Star Trek rerun. Cell phones, streaming music and movies, video chat… who could have imagined it? To some of my hi-tech friends, I'm viewed as a bit of a dinosaur and sometimes described as "old school". I still like writing lists with pen and paper as well as many other antiquated ways of getting things done and keeping my life organized. I really don't mind it much and have resigned myself to the fact that old school sounds decidedly better than simply "old". As resistant to technology as I may be in some ways, even I have embraced certain aspects of it. I can hardly imagine trying to write this book on a manual typewriter armed only with a stack of blank paper and an endless supply of white-out. If you don't know what white-out is, you can look it up... in the encyclopedia.

Technology has changed our lives forever and made so many tasks easier, faster, and more efficient. It has also contributed to making our lives safer. There are numerous devices that can help protect us from harm including burglar alarms, security cameras, and even collision avoidance systems on our cars. In this chapter, I'd like to take a few moments to discuss some of the technological products designed to enhance your safety that are available to anyone, including of course, real estate agents.

One of the most basic personal safety products that has been available on the market for quite some time is the hand-held portable alarm, or noise maker. These devices are simple yet effective as most criminals will not want to stick around while a piercing alarm is blaring and alerting anyone within earshot that you are in need of assistance. One drawback of this type of gadget is that it is only useful if there are people around to hear it. As I have stated earlier, a predator will always seek privacy and seclusion to carry out his crime and a personal alarm may not be loud enough to be heard if you are inside a car or house.

In this day and age, just about every adult carries a smartphone and the "apps" that we install on them are the way that technology helps to make our lives more convenient, productive, and for our purposes, safer. There are a wide variety of personal safety apps available on the market that are compatible with Apple iOS and Android devices. Some are totally free while others may have an upfront cost and/or require an annual or monthly subscription. Of these applications, some are designed for anyone concerned with their own personal safety, while others are tailored specifically for real estate agents and people whose jobs require them to work alone.

Personal safety apps can have a wide variety of features and the specific purposes of those features are varied as well. They are all geared towards keeping the user safe, but some features are more focused on prevention while others do more to document what has occurred and help locate a victim after a crime has been committed. I prefer the products that address both of these concerns but prevention is always the most important objective.

There are many apps available that are designed to enhance your personal safety, and that list continues to grow by the day. For that reason, I am not going to discuss any particular brand or product as they tend to become obsolete very quickly and are constantly being replaced by better and more effective technology. Instead, I will cover some of the many features that these apps provide. To keep this information current, I will continue to post information and reviews of the latest tech products available on my Facebook page at www.facebook.com/prospectorpredator.

Personal Alarm - Some apps can generate a very loud noise, much like the handheld personal alarms described earlier. They can generate a piercing sound in the 120 decibel range. For comparison, that is at about the same level as an ambulance siren. You know how loud they sound when they go driving by but imagine standing right next to one while the siren was blaring.

Mobile tracking - Many apps use a global positioning system (GPS) to track your location in real time. This can enable a buddy, family member, coworker, or someone at your office, to know exactly where you are at any given time.

Video Recording - Some products will record from your smartphone creating a visual record of exactly what is taking place at any time the app is activated.

Video Broadcasting - Far better than simply recording what's taking place, some apps will broadcast live to people that you select or to a monitoring service. (Usually requires a monthly or annual subscription.) This enables the people in your group to become virtual witnesses if you should ever be confronted by a criminal. This can also prevent a crime as the assailant becomes aware that his likeness is being broadcast to another location.

Automated Messaging - This feature will send an SMS text message to the people that you have designated or to the police in the event that you fail to respond to certain prompts or check in at predetermined times. It can include location info by using GPS as well.

Bluetooth Accessories - One type of product that I think is very valuable is a wearable device. This is affixed to the front of your clothing, on a lapel, for example. It can incorporate a camera that can monitor what is happening in front of you much like the body-cams that police officers wear. Some types also have a panic button. The unit is wirelessly connected to your smartphone via Bluetooth technology and can activate the safety app remotely. This type of device can be a great feature to help keep you safe while showing property or conducting an open house.

Hold and release feature - Obviously, in a life-threatening situation, it might be hard to activate an app even if you had the presence of mind to take your phone out in advance and carry it in your hand. Rather than having to press a button on the screen to activate the emergency features, many apps require you to press and hold a button in advance and release it in case of emergency. This way, the alert would be sent even if someone were to take you by surprise or knock the phone from your hand.

Check-in feature - This requires you to check-in with your designated group at certain pre-determined times to ensure that you arrive and depart from appointments safely. It is a great enhancement to the buddy system but it should not be relied upon solely as people are only made aware that there is a problem after it becomes apparent that you are unaccounted for.

Fake phone calls - Some apps can be set up to call you to give the illusion that you are in constant contact with others.

Background checker - Some products allow you to verify the identity of a potential client and do a basic background check to make sure that they are on the up and up. Most legitimate home buyers will not have a problem providing you with ID or being checked out, especially if you tell them that it is a company-wide program intended to keep agents safe. If someone does have an issue with this, it might be a red flag.

Whatever type of product you may consider, I would suggest that you research them collectively as a group with your fellow real estate agents. It is much more effective if the company decides on a particular app for all agents to use. If you are the sole user of a particular app, you may be very familiar with how it works but your emergency contacts may not be. That could end up costing you valuable time, and when it comes to personal safety, minutes and even seconds count.

FRIENDS 12

I don't think anyone could have ever imagined the intricate role that social media would come to play in our society. It is a phenomenon that has evolved rather quickly, but it's hard to imagine a time when it wasn't a part of our everyday lives. While there is some debate as to who originally coined the term "social media", it's one that didn't even exist in the not so distant past. That was back in an age before the word "friend" was a verb and when something going "viral" was definitely a bad thing and cause for a strong round of antibiotics. I doubt that even Mark Zuckerberg, the 19-year-old Harvard student who created Facebook in 2004, could have envisioned the extent that social media has become a part of our American culture.

If you haven't already jumped onto the social media bandwagon, then you are certainly behind the times, and if you haven't embraced it as a powerful tool to help grow your real estate business, you are definitely missing the boat. If you're a savvy agent, I'm sure you've already discovered the power of utilizing social media as part of your marketing and promotional campaigns, as well as for basic name recognition. In the simplest terms, social media allows anyone to reach a vast audience with little or even no expense.

In the early days of the world wide web, a website was something that required considerable cost and expertise to incorporate into your business. Now, that's not only easy to do, but websites themselves have become somewhat unnecessary as Facebook can provide a free platform to promote any product, service, or cause. In days gone by, creating a television commercial was also something reserved for those with substantial marketing budgets, but now anyone with a smartphone that has decent recording capabilities can produce impressive video content. Additionally, there's no need to pay for expensive TV airtime when your videos can be hosted for free on sites like YouTube and displayed on Facebook or any other web-based platform.

Social media can be used for a variety of purposes. It can make someone famous, (or notorious) raise money, sway popular opinion, and destroy reputations. If you have any doubt as to the immeasurable power that social media wields, consider this fact. The Ice Bucket Challenge has raised over 100 million dollars for The ALS Foundation since it first went viral in mid-2013. That staggering amount of money has funded research that will hopefully move scientists closer to a cure for this debilitating disease. In the world of politics, the 2016 Presidential election was absolutely affected by social media and the outcome may or may not have been altered, depending on which cable news network you prefer to watch.

Like many things in life, social media can also be used for less than noble purposes. Shakespeare once wrote, "There is nothing either good or bad, but thinking makes it so". Just as a gun can be used to make war or to keep the peace, the nature of the outcome depends greatly on the intent. For most of us, the internet and social media specifically, can be used for a variety of purposes ranging from business to pleasure. Beyond the professional advantages described earlier, many people utilize social media simply as a form of entertainment. One of the aspects of sites like Facebook that most people find so enjoyable is the ease of communicating with friends and family. It's always great to reconnect with old friends that we had lost touch with long ago. The interaction that takes place within the social media community is usually a result of the information that we share. You share your "likes", opinions, photos, interests, activities, and innermost feelings on your Facebook page, potentially for all the world to see. And therein lies the problem. While your legitimate contacts may find it interesting (or maybe not so much) to see your activity, your comings and goings may be of far greater interest to someone with malicious intent.

We all have a variety of contacts when it comes to sites like Facebook. Some may be family members or lifelong friends, while others are casual acquaintances that perhaps we've only met once. If you use your account for business purposes, you will probably have many contacts with whom you have never spoken but who may represent a future business opportunity. The posting activity of all of these "friends" can be as varied as the people themselves, ranging from the very occasional poster to those who feel the need to keep us all informed of their every meal, workout, pimple or pedicure. An individual's posts, whether they are infrequent or incessant, offer a glimpse into their personal life. Again, that information in and of itself is generally benign in nature, but the intentions of those who view it may not be.

People will often "check in" at specific locations, which may be mildly interesting to some, but to a clever burglar, that information may be far more valuable. The fact that the entire family is in Charleston for Jeremy's soccer tournament this weekend not only announces where you are, but more importantly, where you are not, and that is at home. To a stalker, your constant workout posts may not only give him your schedule but perhaps the name and location of your gym. You know, the one with the poorly lit parking lot?

Everyone has an internal mechanism, a threat meter if you will, that alerts us to potential danger. Some of it is our ever vigilant instinct of survival, and some of it just comes from good old fashioned common sense. Obviously, your perceived threat level varies constantly and is dictated by the circumstances around you, but your instincts are not infallible. There are always hidden dangers that you may be totally unaware of.

One of the common themes of this book is that bad things happen when we are less than alert and our guard is down. You don't need to spend your life in a constant state of paranoia to be safe, but simple awareness and the recognition that threats do exist will keep you far more protected. While you may feel most secure while in the privacy of your own home, you may still be vulnerable and danger may be lurking as close as your laptop or smartphone. As with most potential threats, simple preventative measures can go a long way towards keeping you safe.

The exposure to risk that results from social media activity obviously stems from the information that you share, whether it be shared intentionally or otherwise. That being said, it's also safe to say that your vulnerability generally falls into two categories - the content of what you share and the audience that you allow to see it. Now, it might seem that you could sidestep some of that risk by addressing just one of those vulnerabilities, but that approach is far from foolproof. For example, if you never posted anything that could be used in a malicious way, it wouldn't matter who was able to see it. Alternatively, if you were to strictly limit who could view your posts to those whom you absolutely trust, the content of your posts would be inconsequential.

Some people have never given serious thought to social media safety, while others have found a false sense of security by focusing at least some attention on one of those two areas of concern. I guarantee you that some sensitive information will slip through the cracks regardless of how careful you are with your posts. Additionally, simply limiting your audience to trusted friends is no guarantee that your posts won't be viewed by some shady characters. There are just too many backdoors and roundabout ways that someone can gain access to your profile, your pictures, and your posts. To truly protect yourself while interacting with others online, it is imperative to take a more comprehensive approach.

There is a long list of social media sites available and that list is constantly growing. For our purposes, I will often reference Facebook as its billion-plus users make it the most commonly used platform. Let's start by looking at your own profile and examining what information you have shared. Take a look at your posts, your pictures, and the information shared in the "About" section. Try to look beyond the obvious and think like a predator. What information might be gleaned from what you see? This can be difficult to do as your posts are familiar and their intent is very obvious to you. To continue this exercise, go through the same steps while looking at a friends profile. Finally, move on to a stranger's profile, perhaps a friend of a friend. Try to find the hidden information contained within their posts and pictures. You should begin to recognize just how much you can discover about someone by way of simple observation.

You can learn a great deal about most people from their social media persona. The sensitive nature of some information should seem quite obvious, but not all of what people share will seem risky when taken at face value. A skilled investigator can extrapolate a great deal of data on a person as one piece of information leads to another and then another. On the flip side, a criminal can be equally persistent, and stalkers tend to be particularly obsessive in nature. It can often take just one seemingly harmless photo or post to expose a great deal of additional information. The fact that you regularly check in at the Pilates studio coupled with that photo of you proudly standing next to your new car can make it very easy for a predator to confirm your whereabouts by simply cruising the parking lot. As creepy as all of this may sound, once a stalker "picks up the trail", so to speak, he can follow you, and that will lead to your home, your workplace, and everywhere else that you may lead him.

Maybe I have a suspicious way of looking at things, or perhaps I've just been doing this for too long, but sometimes I see something posted on friend's page that jumps out at me as a big red flag. One example of this is the smartphone app for runners that not only tracks your distance but also shows your route and progress on a map. This information is then automatically posted on your Facebook timeline. People run early in the morning or in the evening, sometimes on running trails or in parks that can be quite desolate. They also tend to have a routine or schedule, so tracking one of these joggers down would not be that difficult if one had access to your profile. Food for thought, and another good reason to read the chapter devoted to pepper spray.

As you review all of your existing social media information, eliminate anything that you feel might expose too much. Additionally, you need to get in the habit of scrutinizing each piece of information that you share before you press the "post" or "publish" button. This may sound tedious, but I assure you it will become second nature in time. Personally, I avoid "checking in" anywhere and I suggest that you do the same. There's plenty of time for that later. You may also want to consider posting pictures and the like after the fact, instead of in real time. It is much more prudent to share those awesome vacation photos once you have returned home.

Now that you have taken the time to examine what you post, it's time to consider who can see your activity. This is something that is so often overlooked, leaving a great deal of information available for anyone to view. Review your privacy and security settings and look for the tabs that control who can see your posts. You will also want to prevent others from being able to "tag" you or post on your timeline without your approval. If you can't seem to find what you are looking for in the settings or help section, consider asking the infinitely wise Professor Google, perhaps he can help. If all else fails, ask a teenager. They seem to know the latest ins and outs when it comes to social media and if you happen to have kids, they can literally be your in-house IT specialists. In addition, be sure to have a secure password and to change it on a regular basis. No birthdays or kid's names, please!

One trend I have noticed among savvy teens, especially girls, is the practice of using a first and middle name only with no last name. It makes it far more difficult for someone to track you down. If you use social media for commercial purposes, consider creating a secondary profile exclusively to interact with business contacts. Aside from keeping your personal profile private, it will keep your professional profile more, well... professional. As a real estate agent, it would be to your advantage to accept friend requests from everyone as they represent potential clients. When you have a business profile, you can feel free to do that as nothing sensitive will appear on that account. You will still have the ability to be more discriminating when it comes to who you interact with on your personal page.

I have purposely written this chapter in somewhat general terms and not gone through any step by step instructions about drop-down menus, tabs, etc. There are so many different social media platforms out there and each has its own unique security and privacy features. Whether you're on Facebook, Instagram, Snapchat, Flicker, Linkedin or some other venue, make sure that you understand how to use the safety precautions provided by the sites that you frequent. It's also important to review those settings on a regular basis as they tend to change quite often.

In conclusion, and in an act of shameless self-promotion, please take a moment to like MY Facebook page at www.facebook.com/prospectorpredator to keep up to date on the latest in safety and security for the real estate professional. Go ahead, I'll wait...

STALKING   13

Stalking has become a commonly used term to characterize certain types of behavior involving varying degrees of threat. It might be used to describe the guy who keeps looking your way from across the bar to serious deviant behavior that can lead to violence and even murder. Whether it be a relatively harmless infatuation or a pathological obsession, most stalkers will share very similar characteristics. Stalking is best described as a sustained pattern of unwanted, obsessive, attention directed towards a specific individual, by another. Many definitions include a qualifier that the actions of the stalker are such that they would evoke fear from a reasonable person, but that would require that the victim be aware of the stalking activity, and that is not always the case. Listed below are various types of behavior that can be categorized as stalking.

- Repeated and unwelcome contact with the victim in person or via telephone.
- Repeated and unwelcome contact by email, text message, mail, or by leaving the victim notes.
- Sending the victim unwanted items or gifts.
- Following the victim or showing up at places that the victim is known to frequent.
- Threatening (directly or indirectly) to harm the victim, the victim's family, or friends.
- Vandalizing or otherwise damaging the victim's home, car, or other property.
- Harassing the victim via the internet.
- Spreading malicious rumors about the victim either verbally or in written form.
- Obtaining personal information about the victim on his own or by hiring a private investigator to do so on his behalf.

While this list is far from all inclusive, you can see that there is a definite pattern to the behavior. In my opinion, the three key elements of stalking are that the behavior is unwanted, obsessive, and sustained. To more fully understand stalking and to be better prepared to recognize concerning behavior, we must first analyze the motivation of a stalker. Motive is the basis for understanding any action. Everything we do in life has a corresponding reason behind it. We go to work to earn a living so that we can afford to purchase the things required for our survival. We go to the grocery store because we need food to sustain ourselves. Behind each and every action that a human being takes there are one or more basic motivations. When distilled down to their most simple form, these motives usually fall into two categories, the seeking of pleasure and the avoidance of pain. Occasionally, these actions can fulfill both of those motivations simultaneously. While I may go grocery shopping to avoid the pain of hunger or even malnourishment, the quart of Ben & Jerry's Chunky Monkey that finds its way into my cart is definitely motivated by my desire for pleasure.

Stalkers derive pleasure in abnormal ways, but their motivations and objectives can be used to define the different types of stalking. They generally fall into the five basic categories listed below, and while some are certainly more dangerous than others, any stalking behavior should be considered deviant and not taken lightly.

The Rejected Stalker - This type of stalker is a former romantic partner or even spouse and his behavior is born from feelings of rejection. The relationship may have been brief or lasted for many years. The stalker often believes that the relationship should never have ended and that a reconciliation is inevitable. If the relationship was short term, he would have likely believed that it was more serious in nature than the victim did. He obviously will not have taken the break up well and may have become volatile. Jealousy can also play a part in this type of behavior as the stalker comes to realize that his former partner has moved on and is seeing other people. It's sometimes easier to understand the mindset of this type of stalker because he is a known quantity. The victim has the added insight into his personality resulting from the experience of the past relationship. This person might have exhibited telling behavior throughout the relationship that contributed to the breakup. He may have been controlling, possessive, narcissistic, or even abusive. In the mind of a warped individual, the stalking can represent a continuation of the relationship as he is unable to face the fact that it is over.

The Resentful Stalker - This type of stalker is not seeking a relationship with his victim. His motive is simply revenge and he will derive pleasure by causing fear and anxiety. It is also a way of exercising power and control. The resentful stalker will often see himself as the victim and believe that his actions are totally justified. In his mind, the actual victim is deserving of the fear they are experiencing. They believe that they have been humiliated, mistreated, or wronged in some way by the victim. The offense may have been real or imagined, but the perceived misdeed will usually be blown way out of proportion. It may have been as simple as being turned down for a date or a dance, or something in a totally different context. The stalker may interact with his target on a professional level. He could be a coworker, the clerk at the dry cleaners, the UPS man, or any of the countless people that we briefly interact with on a regular basis. His actions may be rooted in a sense that "she thinks she's too good for me", with the intent to knock the victim down a few pegs.

The Intimacy Seeking Stalker - This type of individual acts out of loneliness and a desire to enter into a romantic relationship with the subject. His stalking behavior is a way to feel close to his victim and develop a sense of intimacy, even though the object of his affection is often totally unaware of this activity. He will usually lack the proper social skills required to develop relationships in the normal way and will almost always be somewhat of a loner as he is incapable of carrying on relationships with people, romantic or otherwise. His life lacks emotional connection and his behavior may stem from a serious mental disorder. While the resentful stalker will misinterpret a benign gesture as somehow offensive, the intimacy seeker will sometimes read more into your common courtesy. He will often think that the feelings he is experiencing are mutual. He may appear to be shy and basically harmless, but he should not be underestimated. He will seem rather mild-mannered but can become volatile if faced with the reality that his feelings are not reciprocated. You may have friendly interactions with him on a weekly or even daily basis, at a store where he works, for example, but his demeanor might change drastically when you show up with a new boyfriend.

The Incompetent Suitor - This type of stalking usually begins as the result of the victim's rejection of the stalker's advances. Unlike the intimacy seeking stalker, he is not looking for a long-term, romantic relationship but rather a casual sexual encounter. He may consider himself quite the ladies' man and believe that he is very skilled in his approach. His victims will usually see his methods in a completely different way, finding him to be incompetent and worthy of ridicule. He will not recognize the obvious signs of distress exhibited by his target, regardless of how conspicuous those signals might be. He is incredibly narcissistic and totally insensitive to the feelings of others. This type of stalker believes that his continued advances will eventually be successful and that his victim is merely playing "hard to get". In the simplest terms, he's the guy who just doesn't take the hint. He might seem to be more of a nuisance than anything, but he should definitely be taken seriously. You will do well to steer clear of this individual as he will be the type who does not take no for an answer and could become aggressive or even forceful under the right circumstances. While he may be extremely persistent for a time, this type of stalker will eventually move on to another target and continue to repeat this pattern throughout his life.

The Predatory Stalker - To this individual, the stalking is more of a method than typology. He stalks to obtain information in furtherance of his eventual goal, an assault. Violent criminals will often target their victims and stalk them for a time prior to the actual attack. While it is partially a means to an end, members of this classification can be very ritualistic and take great pleasure in the process of selection and the stalking of their prey. Obviously, this type of individual is incredibly dangerous as he enters into stalking with the intent to do harm, whereas the other types do not initially plan to hurt anyone and only become potentially violent when the object of their obsession rebuffs them. While they are categorized here, they are first and foremost predators, and the stalking is a secondary element. They are the serial killers and rapists of the world. These individuals can suffer from some sort of extreme psychological disorder and are often labeled as sociopaths.

They lack conscience and empathy and will feel little or no remorse for their actions. As with some other instances of stalking, the predator will be gratified by exercising power and control over his victim.

Some sources will include cyber-stalking as a type, but I tend to disagree. Using the internet and the vast amount of information available on the web is more of a method to gather information that can be used by any type of stalker. If you are not already aware, there is an incredible amount of information available on just about anyone if you know where to look. Stalkers are very obsessive about their victims and can spend countless hours poring through information right from their personal computer. Social media, court records, and property records can all be easily accessed these days and when cross-referenced, they can be used to learn a great deal about just about anyone. If you have never done so before, just try googling your full name. You may be surprised what may pop up. Just as a skilled investigator can gather information and build a profile on a subject, a stalker can do the same. Each small piece of information can lead to another, and then another.

A stalker's intent may be to use the information he gathers to find a path towards furthering the perceived relationship. The information he uncovers could be used as a topic of conversation or common interest the next time you run into him. He may follow you so that he can plan what at face value seems to be a chance encounter. Your likes and dislikes become valuable information for someone who is trying to win you over. It's a nice quality when people take an interest but beware of those who take too great of an interest or ask too many questions. Just as a stalker believes that knowledge of his victim creates the illusion of intimacy, he may also be overly eager to tell you about himself. The bottom line is to trust your instincts. We have all encountered people that for some reason raise a red flag. The person who is a little too friendly or the guy who seems nice enough but just gives you the creeps.

One common trait among many types of stalkers is that they will often be driven by the desire for love and acceptance, which taken at face value is a rather normal and understandable motive. Where the stalker differs from most is in the methods that he or she uses to try to achieve it. While the average person will take a more typical and straightforward approach, the stalker's desires are often hampered by underdeveloped social skills or his own shortcomings, whether real or merely imagined. He will usually compensate for his lack of self-confidence by admiring his victim from afar, at least at first.

A stalker can spend hour upon hour obsessing over his subject and in a twisted way feels that getting to know more about the person creates a relationship of sorts. Think about the people that you are closest with. They may all be quite different but they share several common elements. Most importantly, they know you well. They may know the intimate details of your life, your likes and dislikes, and what makes you tick. Of course, a stalker discovers the details about you in a warped and clandestine way, but nonetheless, he believes that this knowledge creates a connection or sense of intimacy with his victim.

A stalker will often be at least somewhat delusional as to the relationship that exists between himself and his victim. He may truly believe that he is "in love", even though the object of his affection may only be a very casual acquaintance or even a stranger. While victim and stalker may have never formally met, they have probably interacted at some point or another. This contrived view of some perceived relationship is quite common, and a stalker will often believe that the two are destined to be together. He may be a customer, a co-worker, or neighbor that you have interacted with to some degree, and to the delusional individual, your friendly smile or politeness may be misconstrued as romantic interest.

If you should ever become aware of or even think that you may be a victim of stalking, do not hesitate to contact the authorities. While the legal requirements that constitute stalking vary by jurisdiction, all states have some type of anti-stalking legislation on the books. Most victims will initially claim that they have no idea who might be behind the stalking, but I can virtually guarantee that they know who this person is in one way or another, no matter how casual the connection. He did not choose his victim at random. He has interacted with that person at some point and has obviously taken an interest, albeit an unhealthy one.

BY THE NUMBERS

7.5 MILLION people fall victim to stalking in the United States each year.

Female victims outnumber their male counterparts by a margin of over **TWO TO ONE**.

Approximately **61%** of female victims and **44%** of male victims were stalked by a current or former intimate partner.

An estimated **15%** of women and **6%** of men have reported being a victim of stalking at some point during their lifetime.

Source: The National Center for Victims of Crime

THE OFFICE   14

When you work for a company, you know that over time, your office becomes far more than a place of business. It can become a second home for some, and those who started out as merely co-workers can become friends and even feel like family at times. I think this is true of most businesses and is very much the case when it comes to a realty office. It can truly develop into a community, one filled with a variety of characters, successes, trials, and tribulations. When you think about it, you might spend as much time with your coworkers as you do with family or friends. You may celebrate birthdays, travel to conferences, see each other through marriages and divorces, and even mourn losses together. You're not alone in your real estate career, and I'm sure you know what a tremendous asset your second family can be. This is not only the case when it comes to your success and productivity, but also with respect to your safety and security.

Imagine trying to accomplish everything you do in your real estate career on your own. It can be challenging enough, even with all of the resources available to you. Fortunately, you do have the support of others, and the same holds true when it comes to your safety. Your broker, parent company, as well as your national, state, and local Realtor® Associations all care deeply about your well being. The people who comprise these organizations share the same safety concerns that you do, and more often than not, have put procedures in place to help protect you, the agent. Some organizations have rather comprehensive safety programs in place, while others may be lagging behind, but every broker and agent has the opportunity, and even the responsibility, to contribute to this cause and promote a culture of safety awareness.

This can be accomplished in many ways. Most importantly, it needs to be an ongoing part of everyday life within the agent community, and not just the hot topic of discussion when an incident occurs locally. Knowledge is a key element to any security program and is obviously the reason that I have taken the time to write this book, but your continuing education and awareness are equally important. In law enforcement, you might think that an inexperienced rookie cop would be at greater risk than a veteran officer, but statistics show that is not always the case. While the recent academy graduate cutting his teeth on the streets for the first time may lack experience, his training is recent and procedure is usually more strictly adhered to. The police officer with years of experience under his belt may become more complacent over time, and sadly, his or her life may be at greater risk. The same holds true to your safety. If you read this book only to toss it in a drawer and never think about this topic again, the information contained herein will fade and eventually disappear from your consciousness. Now, I am not suggesting that you read my book on a monthly basis, even I will admit that would become rather monotonous. However, there are plenty of ways to cultivate a culture of safety within your professional community.

If you have been an agent for more than a couple of years, you are certainly familiar with the term "continuing education". While you may find your CE to be a tedious requirement to keep your license up to date, you must admit that it serves a valuable purpose. Similarly, your safety training must be an ongoing process. You may not be aware of just how much information is available to you from various sources. September of each year is designated as Realtor® Safety Month by the National Association of Realtors®, and you will see quite a bit of attention devoted to this topic in your newsletters and trade journals during that time. It's important to continue that deliberate focus after the month has ended and throughout the year. Most offices have weekly and/or monthly meetings and that would provide an ideal format to address agent safety. It can simply be a brief five-minute presentation or discussion on a specific topic, enough to keep safety at the forefront. Probably the most effective dialogue that can take place comes when agents are encouraged to share their own personal experiences, as most have felt unsafe at one time or another.

There are also a great many outside resources that can be drawn from to continue your education. Police officers, security consultants, and self-protection instructors will usually be willing to come by and speak to your group. If they won't come to you, consider going to them. You should take advantage of the opportunities that may already exist as these experts often make presentations at your local association or for other groups such as the Rotary or Chamber of Commerce. If a group of agents is interested in learning more about self-protection, perhaps you could arrange for a group lesson or lessons.

Once safety becomes a priority in your office, it will be easy to begin to implement procedures to keep each other safe. While these procedures need to be adhered to in order to be effective, they shouldn't be set in stone. Quite the contrary, they should always be evolving and improving, and agents should be encouraged to contribute their feelings and ideas so that the safety program will consistently be getting better. With that in mind, the following procedures should be viewed as general guidelines that can be tailored to fit your office and the agents who work there. Additionally, this list is far from complete as I constantly get excellent suggestions from working agents and brokers.

The first area of consideration should be the procedures taken when clients visit your place of business. Your office should have a receptionist or an agent working at the front desk so that anyone entering the building is greeted and assisted with their needs. This is, of course, good for business, but it also controls physical access to the building. A sign in sheet is also an excellent idea to monitor the comings and goings at the office. Once a visitor arrives, they should not be allowed to wander freely about the building. The appropriate agent or employee should be called or paged to the front desk to meet the client and escort them back. The reception area should be the only unlocked access to the building and rear doors and fire exits should remain secured at all times.

The reception area can also be an excellent starting point for many safety procedures. Think of it as the central dispatch of a police department, keeping track of everyone's location and activity. A check in/check out log can be managed so that agent's whereabouts are known, and the receptionist can be contacted by phone to be updated. Without such a system in place, hours or even days can pass where no one knows that an agent might be unaccounted for.

Aside from using the receptionist approach, agents are always encouraged to utilize a buddy system with a coworker. This tried and true method has been around for quite some time and is simple yet effective. While you may prefer checking in with a fellow agent, the office should know who your "buddy" is in case they are unable to reach you directly. These type of check-in systems may seem a bit cumbersome at first, but it will become second nature very quickly. It's just a matter of good communication.

Another safety procedure that I highly recommend is to have an office-wide distress code. This consists of a word or phrase that everyone in the office understands is indicative of trouble but will not be known to an outsider or assailant. Some agencies use the term "Red Folder" as an alert for danger, "Yellow Folder" indicating that there is a cause for concern, and "Green Folder" to signal that all is okay. This can be used by phone, over an intercom system, or in person, to alert other agents of a potential problem.

While most of the dangers that agents are exposed to occur outside of the office, the area of most concern while at your workplace is when meeting a prospect after hours or on the weekend. As much as we would like to limit interactions with clients to regular business hours, that is not always practical as people have jobs and families, not to mention countless other responsibilities to schedule around. You may also find yourself working late and being alone in the building, so you must take extra precautions as that is the time that you are at greater risk. It might be wiser to take paperwork home with you, but if you do find yourself burning the midnight oil, here are some precautions that you can take. The first and best step is to simply not be alone. Perhaps you can plan to stay late on a night when a co-worker is doing the same, and you can absolutely ask a buddy to remain after hours if you are meeting a potential client. You should also keep in mind where your vehicle is parked. If you got the last parking space in the far reaches of the lot earlier in the day, you will want to move it to a spot closer to the door if you will be leaving late. As always, be alert and aware when leaving the building.

Once the office is closed, the building itself should be secured so that people cannot just come in off the street. A real estate office with the lights on and a single car in the parking lot might be enticing to a would be criminal. If you do find yourself in the office alone to meet a client, you can always pretend that someone else is in the building. Leave other office lights on and you can certainly add to the illusion with a creative phone call.

"Hey John, are you going to be here for a while? Okay, I'll see you before I leave."

When it comes to office procedures, it is important to consider the office itself as a key element to keeping agents safe. Building security should be the foundation of your office safety program. Good lighting has long since been considered the simplest and most cost-effective way to deter crime. The perimeter of the building should be well lit with an emphasis on the entrance and employee parking area. An alarm system is also a wise investment for any business, and alarm company signs and/or window stickers will help to encourage criminals to move on to a softer target. Stationary panic buttons at reception and other key locations throughout the building are always a good idea and a portable, wireless, panic button is great for after hours. Beyond an alarm system, security camera systems that were once cost prohibitive for many businesses have become much more affordable. The parking area, main entrance, and lobby/reception area are all excellent locations for cameras. They should be mounted in conspicuous locations and exterior cameras should be placed high enough so as not to be tampered with.

One other area of concern that should be addressed at an organizational level is that of marketing. More often than not, individual advertising is understandably left to each agent. That being said, I strongly suggest that a set of marketing guidelines be implemented and that agents are encouraged to follow them. Time and time again, I see real estate agent marketing materials that feature glamour photography and that provide far more personal information than is necessary. Now, don't get me wrong, an assault is never the fault of the victim, but it is important to keep your professional image just that, professional. The same holds true for any social media accounts that you use for business purposes. You may also want to consider keeping your professional contact info completely separate from your personal information.

Throughout this book, we will focus on interacting with strangers as they are whom we perceive as posing the greatest threat. With that in mind, it is important to consider what point we stop thinking of someone as a stranger. In this day and age, we've become so reliant on remote communication that we are often fooled into thinking that we *know* someone when we really don't know anything about them. So much business is conducted by way of the internet that we take it for granted and confuse this familiarity with actually knowing a person. It has become much easier to relax and trust someone because we have had multiple contacts with them by phone, text, or email. A predator will use this to his advantage and often lean on non-personal communication to promote that feeling of familiarity and encourage you to let your guard down.

In closing, the best and absolutely most effective office procedure that you can integrate into your day to day business activities is to simply keep the conversation going. Remind each other, communicate with one another, and share your concerns and experiences. If everyone is alert and aware and has each other's backs, the vulnerability of every real estate agent will be drastically reduced

OFFICE SAFETY CHECKLIST

Keep the building secure and use only one point of entry. The entrance should be manned by an employee and all other doors should only be able to be opened from the inside.

Know the layout of your building including the nearest unlocked exit(s).

Have multiple escape routes planned in the event of a fire or other emergency.

Be familiar with the alarm system if the office is so equipped and know the locations of panic buttons.

Avoid working after hours. If it is absolutely necessary, have someone stay with you so you will not be alone.

Discuss emergency preparedness at company meetings and create a plan of action.

ACTIVE SHOOTER   15

I had never heard of an "active shooter" when I was growing up in the small suburban town of Cresskill, New Jersey. My school was never on "lockdown" and fire drills were our only effort towards emergency preparedness. Obviously, times have changed and so has the world we live and work in. Active shooter incidents are reported on our evening news on a far too frequent basis. Schools, government buildings, shopping malls, and private businesses, are all potential targets. Sadly, not even an elementary school is immune to attack from what is nothing short of domestic terrorism. I'm sure we could discuss at great length the many intricacies of this continuing problem and likely not come close to a valid reason as to what has so drastically changed in our society to cause this epidemic of mass shootings, nor be any closer to understanding and solving this ongoing American tragedy. For my part, I can only address preparation and response in the event that you should find yourself in an active shooter situation.

While it may be easy to gain an understanding of a perpetrators mindset and motive after the fact, it can be very difficult to do so beforehand. The rationale, or lack thereof, is usually a bit disjointed and invariably tends to stray from reality. In the mind of a shooter, the sequence of events makes complete sense and his actions are totally justified, but to the sane individual, it is often difficult to comprehend. A common theme as to the motive of such disturbed individuals is one of retribution for being wronged in some way, regardless of whether or not the offense was real or not. Many times, the perceived wrongdoing was carried out by a business or organization and the identities of the individual victims may be inconsequential, at least to the shooter. For this reason, it is impossible to predict the likelihood of a violent incident at any particular location.

Real estate agencies interact with hundreds and even thousands of people and it stands to reason that some of them may be less than happy with their experience. A distressed seller may accept an offer that is lower than what they had hoped for and believe that their agent did not do enough to market the property. The agency may be handling the sale of a property that was lost to foreclosure, leaving behind a very angry former owner. There are countless scenarios that may leave a customer displeased and a disturbed individual angered. Again, these offenses need not be based in reality but may seem legitimate in the mind of a deranged person. The motive may have absolutely nothing to do with the business for that matter and may be the result of a domestic situation between an employee and someone they know. "Sally never would have left me if she wasn't spending so much time at that damned job". The bottom line is that it is impossible to rationalize the thinking of an irrational person. You just never know.

Active shooter incidents usually begin suddenly, without warning, and escalate swiftly. As with all of the potential life-threatening scenarios we will discuss in this book, immediate comprehension of what is taking place is critical to your survival. There simply isn't time for shock and disbelief. You must recognize that a threat exists and take decisive action to protect yourself. Survivors of these attacks often report a misinterpretation of what's happening in the early stages of the incident and only come to understand what has actually occurred some moments later.

Gunshots are often thought to be firecrackers, someone shouting in the office is often thought to be a coworker joking around, and valuable time is wasted until realization sets in. Unfortunately, a typical response to these unrecognized threats is to investigate, often leading victims directly into the line of fire. You must program yourself to respond with caution, even before you have a complete understanding of what's going on. It is a far better option than to hesitate, as the situation will almost always unfold rapidly.

Your first and best option when confronted with a life-threatening situation is always to simply leave. If you hear a commotion, shouting, or what may be gunshots, get up and exit the building immediately. Just to make myself perfectly clear, immediately means hanging up the phone without explanation and leaving your purse or other valuables behind. The window of opportunity to successfully escape may be a brief one, so you must move quickly. It could be the difference between being a witness and being a hostage, or worse yet, a casualty. You may encounter coworkers on your way out and everyone will be asking each other "What's going on?". Your best response is "I don't know, get out of the building, now". Be calm but firm and don't waste valuable time on speculation. You can best serve others by getting out safely, contacting the police, and providing as much information as possible. Keep in mind that you may be the only one in a position to do so. Continue out of the building regardless of whether or not others are willing to follow. You should be familiar with the layout of your building and know the quickest escape route in the event of an active shooter, fire, or other emergency. If you have a general idea of where the threat is located, obviously you should choose a route that takes you in the opposite direction. If you feel that your path of egress is obstructed by the danger, you may consider a window as an alternate mode of escape.

Dial 911 as soon as is possible, whether on the way out or after you have exited the building. Make the call from your cell phone. Do not use a landline inside the building as it will delay your escape. Tell the dispatcher everything you can about the situation and be sure to give the address of the building and what has occurred. You will be asked very specific questions. Remain calm and answer as clearly as possible. If you don't know the answer to a question, just say that you do not know. Don't speculate. All information will be critical to a tactical response to the crisis. Important details to include are the number of shooters, the identity of the shooter(s) if known, a description of the shooter, what weapons did the shooter have, and how many people are in the building. Remember, your observations are important and could save lives.

What I have described above is the best course of action in an active shooter situation, but sometimes escape will not be a viable option. There are many scenarios that would prevent you from leaving the building. The shooter may be located in a place between you and the only exit, or perhaps you just don't know exactly where the shooter is. In this case, the best option can sometimes be to shelter in place. The most suitable location to do so is in an isolated room with only one entrance. Close the door and lock it if possible. It can be barricaded with furniture or anything else of weight to further fortify the door. If you are with others, very heavy furniture can be moved with relative ease. Turn off the lights in the room and silence your cell phone. The best choice may be to silence your phone and then turn it off so there is no chance of it vibrating, which can actually seem incredibly loud in a totally silent room. A shooter will often make his way through a building, engaging people as they are encountered. He is seeking out targets of opportunity and may not take the time to try to enter a locked and possibly empty room. If it seems quiet for a while, you should resist the urge to leave your safe area. Stay quiet and stay in place until help comes to find you as active shooter situations have been known to drag on for hours. When help arrives, be sure that it is truly a first responder on the other side of the door. An officer can slide ID under the door or their identity can be confirmed with the 911 operator.

The final and least desirable option in any active shooter situation is to fight. As they say, desperate times call for desperate measures. The odds of successfully engaging an armed assailant are far from optimal, but it may become your last resort. Most attacks of this kind are perpetrated by a lone gunman and if you are with others, you will have the shooter outnumbered. I realize this might be of little solace when fighting off an armed intruder, but fight you must. Your life may depend on it. Consider what you have available to you as a weapon. You may not have pepper spray or other type of defensive weapon, but keep in mind that just about anything can be used as a weapon. A letter opener, a pen, a heavy knickknack, a lamp, or a pot of hot coffee, are all examples of improvised weapons. Survey what you have at your disposal and use whatever you think will be most effective.

Do not assume that a crisis has ended until you are told by uniformed or credentialed first responders. When you encounter police, it is important to remember that they do not know who you are as many of the details of what has happened may still be unclear. Do not approach or hug rescuers. Keep your hands up and listen to their instructions. Follow directions exactly as every person they encounter must be viewed as a potential threat until deemed otherwise. The primary focus of law enforcement will be to neutralize the suspect and clear the building and they will not stop to tend to the injured until the scene is secure. Once you are out of the building, fully cooperate with police and other emergency personnel. They may frisk you and will want to verify your identity. This is done to safeguard all involved. It is not unheard of for an assailant to attempt to escape by posing as a victim, so everyone must be scrutinized until the situation has stabilized. Answer questions and provide as much factual data to the police as possible. The shooter may still be barricaded or at large, and the information that you provide will be a key component of their response.

Hopefully, this chapter has given you an opportunity to consider what might take place at your workplace should an active shooter strike. As always, preparation and forethought are your best defense. Local police departments are training more and more to prepare for active shooter events and will often be happy to give on-site presentations. There are also several training videos available that can be viewed online and at no cost. Take advantage of these resources and spend a few moments to make a plan. It may seem like an unlikely scenario and that it could never happen in your town, but recent history has shown us that it most certainly can. Columbine, Newtown, San Bernardino, Orlando, Parkland. There's no way of knowing what names will be added next, but I guarantee you that this list will continue to grow.

BY THE NUMBERS

There were **40** active shooter incidents in the United States in the combined years of 2014 and 2015 and the incidents took place in **26 STATES**.

These shootings resulted in **231 CASUALTIES.** They included **92 FATALITIES** and **139 INJURED** (excluding the shooters).

These casualties included **4** killed police officers and **10** wounded as well as **3** unarmed security guards wounded.

Of **42** shooters, **39** were male and **3** were female. **14** shooters were killed by police, **16** committed suicide and **12** were apprehended.

Source: The Department of Homeland Security

"Courage is grace under pressure"
- Ernest Hemingway

THE MINDSET OF SELF-PROTECTION 16

Up until now, much of our focus has been devoted to the preventative measures that you can use to help minimize your exposure to risk. As you have seen, there are countless ways to avoid the situations that might put you in jeopardy. Even while following all of these recommendations and being ever vigilant in regards to your own personal safety, there is no way to completely eliminate the possibility of peril. No matter how hard we try, or how aware we *think* we are, there is always the chance that we will, at some point, be confronted by danger. Not every predator fits the same mold. There are always a couple of wild cards in every deck, and no matter how many precautions are taken, they simply slip through the cracks.

As much as I hope that you have found the previous chapters incredibly useful and make them a part of your daily activities as a real estate agent, I truly hope that the information contained in the pages that follow will never be needed. At this point, we need to shift our focus from prevention to action and consider your options should a threat arise. It's often referred to as the unthinkable, implying that it is somehow beyond our imagination or otherwise inconceivable, but that's not quite accurate. While the actors and the scene may vary greatly, the general plot lines are often very similar. It usually involves an assailant attempting to harm or subdue a victim to achieve his eventual goal, whether it be financially motivated or something far more grim. It is usually just that simple. Perhaps it's something that we prefer not to think about, but consider it we must, no matter how distasteful it may be. To counter violence we must first acknowledge that violence exists and that there is evil in this world. We brush up against it every day without even knowing it, but it is there, close enough to touch and close enough to touch us.

Preparation requires us to not only give a great deal of thought to the violence that could be directed towards us but also come to terms with the concept of committing an act of violence on another. Yes, you read that right. It is counterproductive to sugar coat it and call it anything but what it is. When it comes down to a "him or me" moment, the only way to counter violence is with violence, and in the end, the more violent of two combatants will survive. As members of a civilized society, we struggle with the idea of violence and see it as something inherently bad, but violence is merely a means to an end. It can be used to take a life and to save a life, sometimes simultaneously. Violence can be used for good or for evil purposes, and I can think of no better purpose than to save your own life.

The term "self-defense" has become commonplace when referring to anything involving protecting one's self from violence. There are self-defense classes, self-defense techniques, and self-defense weapons. I guess you could say it's appropriate terminology since we're talking about defending your life, but personally, I think that the idea of self-defense is somewhat flawed. You may have noticed that I avoid this phrase for the most part in favor of the term "self-protection". Maybe I'm splitting hairs, but I strongly believe that in any violent encounter, defensive measures are simply not enough. You must be prepared to be offensive and strike. Sure, you can learn the various ways to break free from a choke hold, but where does that leave you? Still face to face with a threatening individual who will employ another method in an attempt to subdue you or simply become frustrated and escalate the level of violence.

Self-Defense is society's way of taking a civilized approach to personal safety. Most of us are nice people with no inclination towards violence. We have no desire to be violent or inflict pain, and we generally view such behavior as unacceptable. Brutality and violence are for the bad people of the world, a category that we certainly don't fit into. So we go to our self-defense classes to learn how to block a punch and break free from a hold. Afterward, we can all stop off at Starbucks for a latte and talk about how we really kicked some butt tonight. It helps us to feel safe yet civilized, but as I said before, defensive measures are simply not enough. Imagine a football game where one team was on the offensive side and the other on defense for the entire game. Which team do you think would win? To survive a violent encounter you must be prepared to take an offensive approach, to harm someone before they harm you.

At the risk of sounding sexist, women often struggle with the idea of causing harm far more so than men do. As children, young girls played with dolls and developed their nurturing skills while the boys took part in activities often fraught with violence, albeit make-believe. Women seem far better at looking past someone's faults and seeing the good in them. Why else would they put up with us men? It's a beautiful quality really, but it can get in the way when it comes to protecting yourself. The area where a woman's protective instincts rival those of a man is when it comes to protecting their children. I recently saw a surveillance video from a discount store in Florida where a mother ferociously fought off a man who was trying to abduct her child. She went absolutely ballistic on this guy and he did not know what hit him. When faced with a threat to her child, a woman can transform into a very formidable and dangerous person. If you have ever done any hiking or camping, you've probably been told to never disturb a nest. A female of any species will fight to defend her young at all costs, whether it be a bear in the woods, an alligator in a pond, or a mom at the dollar store.

Women need to learn to fight with that same ferocity to defend their own lives as they would to defend their children. After all, a predator is trying to deprive your children or loved ones of your presence, and that is certainly worth fighting for. At times in the past, while working with women who seem unwilling or unable to tap into their own protective instincts, I have provoked them with a threatening statement about their kids. That may sound like a cheap shot, but it's highly effective. If you have a hard time imagining yourself lashing out at someone to defend your life, visualize that same assailant threatening to harm your children. As distasteful of a thought as that may be, it will definitely change your mindset. Violence exists in all people, just under the surface and sometimes stifled by fear, but it is there. We are all capable of violence, we just have different triggers.

Of all the tools and techniques that you can learn about in this book and elsewhere, it is important to remember that your mind is more valuable than any of them. Preparing yourself mentally is critical to surviving an assault, and you have already taken steps to develop the proper mindset by reading this book. Deliberately thinking through a potentially threatening situation before it occurs is by far the most important part of your preparation. You will not have time to figure it all out if a situation arises and turns from suspicious to dangerous. There must be a clear plan as to what you will do if someone becomes a threat. You have to come to terms with the idea that while you are a kind and peaceful person, you will not allow anyone to harm you, and you are willing to do what is necessary to protect yourself. All of the knowledge and skill in the world will be of no help if you are not willing to use it. You have to make a conscious decision here and now. If god forbid you should ever find yourself in a life-threatening situation, you must decide that you will be the one who walks away.

If a criminal simply wants to steal from you, there is nothing wrong with letting him take what he wants and leave. No ring, car, or amount of money, is worth your life. One of the telltale signs that a criminal is financially motivated is that he will move fast, wanting to perpetrate his crime and quickly make his escape. He has no reason to stick around as this jeopardizes the success of his crime. He will take what he wants from you and depart as soon as possible. The predator who lingers usually has something more sinister in mind. The more time he spends, the greater the risk to himself. If he wants to take you to another location, that is an entirely different matter.

In law enforcement, there is a common term known as the "secondary crime scene". While this may seem self-explanatory, there is much more to be said about it beyond the obvious. Of course, this refers to a second location where a crime continues beyond the original crime scene. In an abduction, for example, a person may be taken from a mall parking lot and then transported to the predator's house which would become the secondary crime scene. Any time a criminal takes someone to another place, the outcome is more often than not tragic. Just the act of taking someone without their consent elevates the crime and indicates that the perpetrator is not particularly concerned about the consequences. If a criminal is inclined to take you somewhere against your will, he is most likely prepared to do just about anything and you must act accordingly. An assailant may assure you that no harm will come to you as long as you go with him peacefully, but statistics have shown that this is rarely the case. The last place that you want to be is at a secondary crime scene. Sadly, people do not often survive the secondary crime scene, and it is a place where heinous things happen. If this all sounds rather disturbing, it should. The point I'm trying to make is that if you ever find yourself in a situation where someone wants to take you elsewhere, that is the time you need to do everything in your power to fight and to survive. You are better off risking your life at the primary crime scene and fighting for your life right then and there than being taken somewhere private and secluded where you will have little hope of escape.

If you should ever become the victim of a crime, there will undoubtedly be a moment when you become acutely aware of that very fact. A moment when you realize you're not just being suspicious or paranoid, this is really happening. It's a sinking feeling when suddenly fear becomes reality and you find yourself in a situation where your safety and possibly your life are in danger. You don't have time to question what you know to be true. Your body and mind need to switch into survival mode. As I have said in earlier chapters, each of us has tremendous survival instincts, and they are incredibly powerful if you embrace them, but you can't waste time in disbelief or on second-guessing yourself. You must shift gears and begin to focus on protecting yourself. Many people shrink from this moment, overcome by fear, and that is understandable. You have taken the initiative to safeguard yourself, so you are not just any person. You are someone who has prepared for this moment, who thought it through and practiced the skills needed to fight back. You must reach down deep and summon those survival instincts. Believe me, they are right there inside of you. You need to fight for everything that's important to you, your family, your children, your very life, because in the end, they all depend on it. You can cower and surrender, or you can fight.

Your heart will be pounding and adrenaline will be pumping through your veins. You've probably heard of adrenaline referred to as the fight or flight hormone. It's aptly named, as these are your only two options. Many of you may be thinking that you have never been in a physical altercation in your life and are totally unprepared to fight off an assailant. Keep in mind that when I tell you that you have to fight, you only need to buy yourself an opportunity to escape. You're not going to go 15 rounds in a boxing ring with an opponent twice your size. Your objective is to incapacitate your assailant as quickly as possible and leave the scene. It does not take much time to get out of the house and into your car or to a neighbor's house.

An important point to make is the difference between hurting someone and incapacitating them. Pain is a relative term, and everyone has a different threshold. Additionally, drugs or alcohol can drastically change a person's level of tolerance. Pain is something that an assailant can shake off and continue his assault, whereas to incapacitate someone means to render them non-functional and unable to continue. To survive an encounter with a predator, your objective is not to simply hurt them, but to cause injury to the point of incapacitation. Inflicting pain may do little more than enrage an assailant and believe me, he will not have the same hesitation when it comes to harming you. Your attack must be swift and efficient. You don't have the time to strike halfheartedly and wait to see if your methods have had any effect. While violent attacks in the movies are rarely an accurate portrayal, think of how many times you have watched a fictional victim fight back against an assailant, only to be chased down again and eventually subdued. It makes for good drama but also acts as a visual demonstration of the shortcomings of a defensive approach to a threat.

In the 1980s and '90s, our government's response to terrorism could best be categorized as "tit for tat". Each time our country's interests were attacked, we would respond in kind. They bombed our embassy, we would bomb some remote terrorist training camp. The White House press secretary would describe our response with words like "measured" and "proportionate". This approach continued for years until our enemies escalated the level of violence on September 11, 2001. Since that time, the approach has obviously changed, but the war on terror continues to drag on with no end in sight. In a life-threatening encounter, you cannot afford to be measured in your reply. Your response must be disproportionate and overwhelming. Your objective is not to fight someone, your objective is to end the fight. To not only strike but to strike again and again to ensure that your assailant is not only unwilling to continue his assault, but is physically unable to.

I am sure that all of this sounds rather brutal to most of you. Perhaps you were more comfortable thinking of your own survival in the more civilized terms of self-defense. I can assure you that having the knowledge and ability to halt an attacker does not make you a violent person. Quite the contrary, most good people who have the mindset and the skills required to protect themselves seem to have a heightened respect for life and maintain the desire to avoid confrontation at all costs. It can be empowering to know that you have the capability to protect yourself and are willing to do what is necessary to survive, but that empowerment begins with a mindset of survival. When faced with the choice of "him or me", a predator will always choose himself. You must be prepared to do the same.

THE FUNDAMENTALS OF SELF-PROTECTION   17

By reading this book, you have obviously taken the matter of your own personal safety very seriously, and that is certainly to be commended. I also realize that you probably don't have the time nor the inclination to devote an inordinate amount of your life to studying the intricacies of the various forms of martial arts. There are hundreds of unique styles and any one of them can take years, if not a lifetime, to master. It's not necessary, however, to become a black belt in Karate or learn to move with the grace and precision of Bruce Lee in order to protect yourself.

What follows in the coming pages would by no means be considered "martial arts", but there are certain fundamental concepts that are derived from, and are common to, most fighting disciplines. While traditional martial arts require elaborate and sometimes complicated movements, I subscribe to the philosophy of simplicity and always favor the quickest path from point A to point B when it comes to self-protection. It's far from an original concept. Bruce Lee was a pioneer in the art of combat and revolutionized martial arts in the 1960s. While trained in the classical Chinese discipline of Wing Chun, he soon recognized the inadequacies of traditional martial arts which led him to the development of his own style of fighting, Jeet Kune Do, in 1967. It was a departure from the philosophies of other disciplines which had been taught and practiced in the far east for centuries.

Jeet Kune Do was somewhat of a hybrid of many other disciplines, taking the best from each and discarding the rest. Lee stressed what he called "economy of motion" and emphasized the importance of speed and efficiency. While no one will ever confuse me with Bruce Lee, I will try to take that same basic approach here. We will focus on the fastest and most effective way to incapacitate an assailant. The approach is a fairly simple one and while practice is always a good thing, a thorough understanding of the concept is the most important factor.

Before we discuss any actual techniques, I'd like to cover a few basic concepts here. Any coach will tell you that the most fundamental key to your success is just that... the fundamentals. They are what form the foundation for learning any new skill. While these basic principles are the first steps towards becoming proficient, they remain critical long after the student has advanced beyond the beginner level. Even an expert who is extremely knowledgeable in the most expert techniques will struggle if he allows his fundamental skills to falter. While they may seem a little less exciting, they are essential to effective execution.

When it comes to self-protection, the most basic of these concepts is that of stance. So much of what we do physically with our body is literally rooted in our feet and legs. Your stance, or the position of your feet, will dictate how much force you can exert with your upper body. You won't see a boxer squarely standing and facing his opponent. His body will be positioned at roughly a 45-degree angle with his power side farther away from his opponent. For a right-handed fighter, the left foot will be forward and the right foot will be back. If you are left-handed, this would obviously be reversed. This is known as a bladed stance and it accomplishes a few different things. From a defensive standpoint, your vulnerable targets such as your face and torso are angled away from your assailant, offering some measure of protection from a strike. You are also able to move your body more effectively to avoid a being hit from this position. With your strongside back, that leaves your weaker side forward and closer to an attacker. Your left arm and hand, assuming you are right-handed, can be used to block and repel an incoming punch while the right arm is back, cocked and ready to strike.

Throughout this chapter, I will be describing certain motions to you. When prompted, I'd like you to take a moment to get up out of your easy chair and actually go through these motions. Muscle memory is a powerful teaching tool. While understanding these movements is very important, they will have a greater impact if you physically *feel* what I'm talking about. So up and at 'em, on your feet. I want you to stand with your feet at shoulder width, squarely facing forward and towards an imaginary person. Again, you are facing directly forward with both feet at an equal distance from your target. Now, with your feet remaining stationary, visualize that imaginary assailant attempting to hit you in the face. If you move to try to avoid being struck without moving your feet, your only option is to lean back from the waist. For most people, that means moving your face at most about 8 to 12 inches farther away from your assailant before losing your balance and stumbling backward. Now, adjust your position so that your feet are in a bladed stance, facing forward at a 45-degree angle. You will find that you are able to move your

THE FUNDAMENTALS   179

head away from your attacker much more effectively from this position while still maintaining your balance. You should be able to feel the difference between these two reactions to an imagined strike, but stance is not just about defense.

From an offensive point of view, stance and power go hand and hand. Return to a position facing squarely towards your imaginary target and with your dominant hand, pretend to punch that target in the face. Repeat this a few times. Don't feel silly, no one is watching. You will notice that your punch doesn't seem to be very powerful, and you can feel that the motion is being carried out by only your arm and shoulder. Now, shift your feet into a bladed stance and throw that same punch. Focus on using your entire body. Your weight is shifting from your back leg to your front, and your hips and torso are rotating. This is where all power comes from, not just in fighting, but in most sports that require the generation of force. Watch a pitcher in baseball, a football quarterback, or a tennis player serving the ball. You will see the same common component that you see in a boxer throwing a punch. Strongside back, cocked and ready, and then the entire body in motion to drive forward with explosive force.

No discussion about the fundamental benefit of utilizing proper stance would be complete without also discussing the importance of balance. In the event of a confrontation, your feet should always be about shoulder width apart. Too wide or too narrow of a stance will substantially diminish your stability. We spend most of our time on our feet with our knees locked in an upright position. For the most part, that's just fine, but in a situation where you need to protect yourself, it is critical to lower your center of gravity by bending your knees ever so slightly. I'm not talking about dropping into a squatting position or anything like that. Unlocking your knees enough to lower your body a half inch or so is enough if you are in relatively flat shoes. If you wear more of a heel try dropping down just a little more. Bear with me and hop up on your feet again. Standing in your bladed stance, note the difference of bending your knees just a little bit. You will find that your balance is greatly enhanced and you become much more stable. Your center of gravity has lowered and you will be more anchored to the floor. Can you feel it? Imagine someone grabbing you or shoving you. From an upright position you can easily be thrown off balance or knocked down, but with your knees bent just a little, you are far more stable to defend yourself and fight back.

Hopefully, you have taken to your feet and have actually felt how critical proper stance and balance are to self-protection. A house is only as strong as its foundation and the same holds true for the human body. No matter how well you learn to punch or kick, your strike will lack power and be relatively ineffective if you do not apply these most fundamental concepts.

Before moving on to actual technique, I would like to discuss one more very important principle of self-protection. Throughout our upbringing and continuing on into adulthood, we have been taught certain values and rules to be followed during the course of our lives. Certain tenets of civilized society that should always be adhered to. Concepts like honor and a sense of fair play are evident all across our culture and we have consistently been told that we should always fight fair. While these values are very important, they must be abandoned when it comes to defending your life. You must not only ignore the idea of fighting fair but in fact, do the complete opposite and embrace the concept of fighting unfairly. Fairness is fine in a boxing ring but serves no purpose in the world of self-protection, and an unfair advantage is one of your best weapons when faced with an assailant who may be bigger and stronger than you are. When we think of fighting fair, there are a number of cliches that may come to mind. Age old sayings like "No hitting below the belt", "No sucker punches", and "Never kick a person when they're down."

In a civilized society, these all make for good advice, but in a confrontation with a predator, they become the perfect starting point and a list of things that you absolutely should do. So abandon the idea of fighting fair, because in reality, it is not a fight at all, it's an assault, and you must be prepared to respond accordingly.

"In the midst of chaos, there is also opportunity"
- Sun Tzu, The Art of War

THE TACTICS OF SELF-PROTECTION **18**

Now that we have covered the basics, we can move on to the nuts and bolts of self-protection and the physical act of striking someone. If you're like most people, you probably recoiled from that statement just a bit. Perhaps you were more comfortable discussing stance and balance, but the fact remains that in order to stop someone who intends to harm you, you are going to have to strike them in some way, shape, or form. I wish I could tell you that you can just pull this book out of your purse and wave it in front of their face and quietly make your escape, but that is obviously not reality. A predator is not going to simply roll over and play dead. It's up to you to stop him. At some point, he made a deliberate choice to harm you, and chances are, he has harmed others before. He is counting on the fact that he is more prepared than you are because he chose this path a long time ago, probably before he ever made an appointment or even contacted you. He is expecting that you have never contemplated the scenario that is about to unfold and that you have not made any choices of your own. You must make that conscious decision, here and now. If someone ever attempts to do you harm, you will strike them, and you will stop them. If you are still struggling with this concept, I strongly suggest that you re-read the chapter regarding the mindset required to survive an assault. I know that I've mentioned this more than once, but I cannot emphasize it enough. You can learn all of the techniques there are to know, but all of that will be totally useless if you are not willing to use them if the situation warrants it.

One of the most powerful concepts when it comes to actually hitting a someone is the point of focus. Most people would think that if my intent was to hit a person in the nose, I would aim for their nose. Actually, that would be incorrect. If your intent is to hit someone in the nose, the effect of such a punch would be far more devastating if you aim through the target and focused on the back of the head. Your strike should always be focused on a point five or six inches beyond the actual target. Your brain will

THE TACTICS OF SELF-PROTECTION   185

anticipate the impact of your fist striking that nose, and your punch will slow up right before impact. If you have ever seen a martial artist break wooden boards, you will see that his strike drives through the target as opposed to simply hitting it.

With that in mind, let's talk about the mechanics of a strike. Obviously, there are two basic components involved. A part of your body impacting a part of another person's body. The relationship between these two body parts is the determining factor as to how effective, or ineffective, a particular strike will be. If I were to poke you hard in the chest with my pinky, which one of us do you think would sustain more harm? I think it's a safe guess that my pinky would come out on the losing side of that one. Now, sticking with my little finger as my weapon of choice, suppose I targeted the eye? Do you see my point? (at least with your one good eye) This should demonstrate that the connection between weapon and target, and how one impacts the other, is vital to the effectiveness of a strike.

If you have ever done any demolition, or even seen it done on your favorite home improvement show, it's all about using the right tool. I wouldn't get anywhere pounding on a block wall with a screwdriver, but I could definitely do some damage with a sledgehammer. I also might start by striking a weaker part of the wall in order to bring it down. In kind, we must use the most solid weapon at our disposal to impact the weakest target available. Now, you may have noticed that I keep using the word "weapon", and might be wondering if you inadvertently skipped a few pages. Every part of the human body is potentially a weapon, and at the same time, every part of the body is a potential target. Before we start examining the anatomy and its possible targets, let's first inventory the weapons that you have at your disposal.

One common theme that you may notice in my writing is that I will always do my best to lead you away from what we have been programmed to believe in the movies and on television, and towards the techniques that are effective in the real world. What part of the human anatomy do we see used as a weapon, time and time again, in the fictional portrayal of violence? The answer is, of course, the fist. A good old punch to the face can easily be delivered with tremendous force, usually doing substantial damage to the person on the receiving end. At least that's how it's commonly portrayed. The fact of the matter is, for the average person, a punch is an incredibly low percentage strike. A boxer or a martial artist can deliver a great deal of force with a single punch to the face, but that same punch from most people will have little or no stopping power.

THE TACTICS OF SELF-PROTECTION 187

Generating sufficient force to do any damage with a punch is difficult, but certainly not impossible. The far more serious flaw with this choice is your fist's lack of resilience. The human hand is comprised of 27 bones if you count the short carpal bones in the wrist, some no larger in size than a peanut, and they are held together by the soft tissue of muscles, tendons, and ligaments. It is the delicacy of the hand that gives it dexterity and nimbleness but also makes it a poor choice as a striking implement. This fragility makes the hand susceptible to injury and could leave you to figuratively fend off an attack with one hand tied behind your back. If you've ever seen a boxer with his gloves off before or after a fight, you will notice that his hands are heavily taped, forming a protective cast-like covering. They also tape up when working out on a punching bag. Without that protection, their punches would do far more damage to their own hands than to the face and body of their opponent.

I can remember spending my summers as a teenager at the Jersey Shore. The arcades on the boardwalk always had one of those punching bag machines. You know, the kind that you would hit as hard as you could and your strength would be measured on a big dial with adjectives like "wimpy" and "mama's boy" at the lower end of the scale and something like "He-Man" at the top. As if my friends and I needed any more motivation to flaunt our rapidly approaching manhood. I can recall giving it a try once. In all my summers at the shore, that machine only got twenty-five cents from me. I had to wear an ace bandage on my wrist until school reopened in the fall.

At this point, you probably have more questions than answers. You may be thinking; "If not the fist, then what?" and silently hoping that I am not going to explain how to execute a leaping roundhouse kick to the face that will require months to master, not to mention countless hours of stretching exercises. Well, fear not. I promised you simplicity, and my philosophy on what to strike with is very uncomplicated. In the simplest of terms, you want to use a hard and resilient part of your body to strike a softer and less durable part of your attacker's body.

Your knee is a very solid choice and you can deliver a considerable amount of force with it. Compare the prospect of being struck by a knee or a fist, as well as the difference in muscle size between the leg and the arm. The knee can be a powerful weapon, but only if used in the proper context. The effectiveness of each weapon depends greatly on the target that it is used on. Obviously, the knee is more useful in striking the lower half of the body and pairs nicely with the groin. Forgive me if I sound like I am about to recommend a nice wine to go with that. But seriously, the value of both weapon and target will be determined by this "pairing" and the relationship between the two.

If we follow this line of thinking, what other body parts might make a good weapon? The elbow is a fairly hard and structurally sound part of your body, but it may be difficult to use effectively when face to face with an assailant. However, if we simply change the circumstances, it can become an excellent choice. When accosted by someone from behind, your options will be limited, but your elbow might be the best choice. You can generate considerably more force when elbowing someone behind you than you can by punching someone in front of you. The best targets in this scenario are the stomach, ribs, and groin.

Now, you may recall that I was fairly critical of the idea of punching someone with your fist, but that doesn't mean that your hands cannot be used as an effective weapon. For the reasons outlined earlier, the idea of punching someone in the head or torso is not your best option, but the odds shift considerably if we focus that punch on a more vulnerable target like the groin. You should also keep in mind that while the front of the fist and your knuckles are very fragile, other parts of the hand are much more sturdy. The palm is fairly solid and can be used to strike the nose, driving upward from the tip towards the forehead. This is one of the easier ways to break someone's nose. The blade of the hand is also a great choice when striking with a fist. The blade is the meaty area of the hand that runs from the base of the pinky finger down to the wrist. Striking with this part of the hand is sometimes called a "hammer fist" because you will literally use your fist like a hammer. Just pound your closed fist on a table top. The area making contact with the table is the blade of your hand. It is very effective to swing downward from above your head, striking the bridge of your aggressor's nose. You can generate much more power striking this way as opposed to a punching motion, and the risk of disabling yourself is far less. Imagine pounding on someone's front door as loud as you could. I would much prefer doing so with a hammer fist than striking the door with my knuckles.

While your hands naturally pair up well with the face as a target, you should keep in mind that blows to the head are rarely incapacitating. The attacker's face may be the most accessible target, but you should use this type of strike to set up a more devastating blow. Hitting the nose and eyes can stun and even blind a person for a brief moment, giving you an opportunity to follow up. Do not misinterpret that momentary disruption as an opportunity to escape. An assailant will recover quickly from this type of strike and will certainly be able to pursue you.

The next weapons at your disposal are your feet. When you think about it, unless you're showing real estate in the Florida Keys, your shoes are the only hard part of your wardrobe, and your feet are the only protected part of your body. Because of their proximity to the floor, your feet are limited to striking targets in the lower part of the anatomy. Of course, if you are a former Rockette, by all means, feel free to kick his teeth out. As always, the circumstances will dictate which targets and weapons are accessible. If grabbed from behind, driving your heel down onto the assailant's instep can be very painful. Just like strikes to the face, a blow to the foot will cause momentary pain and should be used to buy a second or two to use a more effective tactic.

The foot is probably most effective when used on a person who is on the ground. Oh, was that another cringe? You're thinking of that saying again, "Don't kick a guy when he's down". Well, I have another cliche for you... "He may be down, but he's not out". Believe me, people get up, usually more angry and violent than before. Predators who get up still harm, and rape... and kill. Remember, your objective is not to inflict pain but to incapacitate. While your shoe is the hardest part of your wardrobe, the heel is the hardest part of the shoe. I have seen some of the heels that you ladies wear and they look like pretty formidable weapons. The most powerful strike with the heel is to raise your knee up and drive down with the heel. A person who is down on the ground is vulnerable, and all of their targets are exposed. Driving the heel into the groin, the neck, or the face is a very devastating blow, and will ensure that he will not get back up.

There is one other part of the body that can be used in the right circumstances but is often overlooked. The head can be incredibly hard, at least that's what my mom always told me, and can make an excellent weapon. If someone were to have a hold of you, in close proximity, face to face, a headbutt to the bridge of the nose might be your only available option. Again, this is not a devastating blow, but would definitely stun an assailant and offer an opening to strike again. If someone were to grab you from behind, striking the face with the back of your head might also be possible.

There is a tactic that is less about the weapon and the force generated and more about the vulnerability of the target. The target I'm referring to is the eyes, and I'm sure I don't have to tell you just how sensitive they are. If you're like me, you have been totally incapacitated by a drop of sunblock or an eyelash at one time or another. What makes the human eye such a valuable target in terms of self-protection is that you can deprive an attacker of his sight as well as inflict harm. If your assailant has been blinded, the fight is over for all intents and purposes. If I can use my movie reference one more time, how often have you seen an onscreen victim gouging the eyes of an attacker? Quite often, I assume. You'll notice that the bad guy never seems too fazed by this and just keeps coming. In reality, the eyes are incredibly frail and it does not take much force to drive thumbs into the eyes. Again, I know some of this sounds gruesome, but this may be a matter of life or death.

We've talked a lot about targets and weapons, but as I have said earlier, self-protection is more about grasping the concept of what to do rather than learning and practicing a specific set of movements. A sloppy and uncoordinated strike to the groin has equal value to a graceful arcing roundhouse kick, assuming they both drop the assailant to the ground. No one will be holding up cards and judging your style and technique. Self-protection is graded on results. If a situation becomes violent, your purpose is not to defend. Your assailant is attacking you and you must be prepared to turn the tables and attack as well. You are not to rely on one strike to stop him, it will require multiple blows. Keeping in mind that not all strikes are incapacitating, the best target is the target that is available to you. Each strike creates an opportunity for the next. You should be working towards an incapacitating strike at the earliest opportunity. Once you have that opening, there is no need to stop at one. You don't have the luxury of delivering a strike and then waiting to measure its effectiveness. You cannot leave this to chance. Strike and strike again and again, until you know he is done and you can make your escape. If a strike is effective, do it again. Your progression does not have to be A followed by B followed by C. A followed by A, followed by A again, can be equally effective, if not more so.

I have tried to stick to some very basic concepts in these last chapters on self-protection, but conveying actual technique can be challenging in written format. It's much easier to learn physical skills by seeing them demonstrated and by actually repeating those movements. If you are so inclined, there are many excellent classes available that teach effective self-protection. Do some research and ask around. If you are not interested in that approach, much can be learned by watching techniques demonstrated online, in video format.

ARMED AND DANGEROUS 19

Baseball, hot dogs, apple pie and… Glock? Love 'em or hate 'em, guns are here to stay and they have become an integral part of American culture. There are estimated to be over 340 million firearms in this country. That's one for every man, woman, and child in the United States with enough firepower leftover to start a fairly large scale ground war. We have more guns in America than people and American civilians own an estimated 46% of the non-military firearms in the world.

Of all the chapters that I have written for Prospect or Predator, I would have to say that I've spent the most time contemplating this one. Truth be told, I thought long and hard as to whether or not to even include a chapter on guns as part of this text. There are many complicated topics that fall under the broad heading of firearms. They include but are not limited to, gun ownership, concealed carry, deadly force, as well as shoot-don't-shoot decision making and tactical shooting techniques. And let's not forget the second amendment and our constitutional right to bear arms. There are a great number of books devoted to each of these subjects and I don't feel that I could do any of them justice here in the space of one brief chapter. In the end, I know that for many of you, carrying a handgun for the purpose of self-protection is a serious consideration and this book would not be complete if I did not address this topic. So for our purposes, I will primarily focus this discussion on the decision of whether or not to carry a gun and hopefully give you some valuable food for thought.

Before we go any further, you must first familiarize yourself with the legal aspects of carrying a gun. In some states, legally carrying a firearm is nearly impossible, while in other states, a concealed carry permit can be easily obtained by most any adult who does not have a criminal record or history of mental illness. In my home state of New Jersey, for example, a concealed carry permit was very difficult to obtain, but in my current state of residence, Florida, it is quite simple to do. That being said, I must preface this conversation with the following warning. Do not under any circumstances carry a firearm if you cannot do so within the laws of your state and are fully prepared to follow those laws to the letter. Beyond the obvious legalities, the broader conversation becomes one of moral, societal, and even spiritual implications, not to mention the potential liability involved if you should ever discharge your weapon. So let's examine this more carefully as it is certainly a very serious matter and one that should be given the utmost consideration.

Everyone knows what a gun is, and we've all seen what they can do, at least as it is portrayed on the screen, both large and small. Obviously, the shootouts portrayed there are fictional and in most cases, nothing at all like reality. I'm always amazed at how the bad guys are always dropped with one incredibly accurate shot, even when running and at a great distance, while the hero is only just *grazed*. In the real world, people bleed out and die rather quickly from a wound to the shoulder or leg if the bullet happens to nick the right artery. Another inaccurate and fairly cavalier portrayal is the idea that people can snuff out a life very inconsequentially and seem to move on from the encounter with ease. We've all seen our favorite fictional cops meeting up at the local pub for a cold one after a rough day of killing drug dealers. The reality is, veteran police officers who have taken a human life, and justifiably so, can be haunted by it for the rest of their lives. Being right or justified will not shield a person from the feelings of guilt and remorse, or from second-guessing themselves and their actions. It's only when the dust settles will it be known that even the baddest of bad guys was someone's son, or brother, or father.

To take a more realistic look at what guns and bullets can accomplish, let's first examine the 9mm Luger, or more precisely the 9x19 Parabellum cartridge. It has become the most common and popular type of ammunition for people on the right and wrong side of the law. The cartridge itself is made of brass and accommodates a lead bullet weighing about 115 "grains", the common unit of measurement when it comes to bullets. It is roughly the equivalent to 7 ½ grams or a little over a quarter ounce. Its diameter is approximately 9.01 millimeters, thus the name. Fired from a typical and modern 9mm handgun, this round of ammunition produces about 323 ft/lbs (foot pounds) of energy. Fascinating, huh? Well, perhaps not so much. Maybe it would help if I put it into more *human* terms.

That same little quarter ounce led bullet enters a human body traveling at about 1125 feet per second, depending on the distance from which it was fired. I'll save you the trouble of finding your calculator, that's about 767 miles per hour. It pierces the skin with ease, leaving not much more than a small round hole of, you guessed it, about 9.01 millimeters. But once it enters the body, that's where the real magic happens. It cuts through muscle tissue, cartilage, and internal organs without much resistance, and shatters bone on contact.

Early ammunition merely passed through the body cleanly, without much deflection, and often exited the victim leaving a similarly sized hole on the other side. Manufacturers quickly realized that this was a missed opportunity when it came to stopping power, the ultimate objective of a bullet. More damage would certainly be done if the bullet were to expand within the body, therefore causing considerably more tissue damage and bleeding as well as forcing the body to absorb the full impact as opposed to a bullet that passed directly through. Thus, the hollow point bullet was born. Designed to enter cleanly and expand and mushroom upon impact, and in some instances fragment within the body causing as much internal injury as possible. I remember a case some years back where a bullet was surgically removed from the calf of a victim who had been shot in the arm. If a bullet does manage to exit the body, it can leave a wound many times larger than that of the entrance wound, and often take a proverbial pound or so of flesh with it. My apologies for the graphic nature of the previous description, but I strongly believe that any conversation about carrying a firearm would be grossly inadequate if it did not frankly discuss the physical devastation that one tiny bullet can cause.

Keeping in mind how deadly a gun can be, it should be fairly obvious that carrying one is a tremendous responsibility. That being said, the obligation begins at the moment you purchase a firearm as safeguarding and properly securing that weapon are your first priorities. Most guns are legally purchased and registered, but it is important to remember that legal guns get stolen and wind up killing a great many innocent people each year and wounding countless others. A firearm needs to not only be stored in a safe location, but also be secured itself in the event that it should unintentionally fall into the wrong hands. Most people will keep a gun well hidden in the home, at least in their opinion, but an experienced burglar has probably seen them all, including the most seemingly clever hiding places.

More importantly, if you have children, you know that they tend to see and hear everything. They can be incredibly curious and are great at finding things. So many gun owners will tell you that they keep their gun hidden in a place that is up high and out of reach of children, but kids are natural climbers and can scale a bookcase like Spiderman if they are so inclined or curious enough. You should also keep in mind that other children may be in your home at some point or another. Kids have sleepovers and your friends and relatives have children too. The other kids may be a little older and more capable than your own toddler. The expression "Better to be safe than sorry" could never be more true. There are several locking devices for a firearm readily available. I prefer the combination lock type personally, as keys can be found by the curious and determined just as easily as the gun itself. Ideally, a gun should be well hidden and locked. It is also wise to store your ammunition in a separate and secure location.

Sadly, avoidable incidents take place on a far too frequent basis, often with devastating consequences. Children find their parents guns and bring them to school to show or impress a friend. They have been known to accidentally fire them, injuring or even killing others. Sometimes, and tragically so, they turn a firearm on themselves. The majority of these weapons were legally owned by law abiding citizens. Time and time again, I hear people refer to themselves as "responsible gun owners", but for some, their actions prove that they are anything but.

When handling a firearm, you must always keep in mind that you are holding a deadly weapon. It was designed for the purpose of killing and must be handled with extreme care. Always treat a firearm as if it is loaded, no matter how sure you are that it is not. Countless people have been killed and maimed by guns that were presumed to be empty. For the same reason, you should never point a gun at someone, loaded or otherwise, unless you are prepared to kill them.

While your home is usually a safe and controlled environment, all of that goes out the window when you take that weapon out into the world. I prefer that a handgun be transported on your person, assuming it is legal to do so in your area and you possess the necessary carry permit. Once you place it in a purse or briefcase, you have considerably less control over it. The same goes for transporting a firearm in your vehicle. A gun in your glovebox or console is far too easy to forget about.

Ironically, as I have been writing this chapter over the past several days, a story on the evening news caught my ear. A 31-year-old mother from Jacksonville was shot while driving her vehicle on a Florida highway. The early reports from the Putnam County Sheriff's Department state that she was shot through the seat of her car by her four-year-old child. The toddler had apparently gotten hold of the woman's .45 caliber handgun in the back seat. The woman is reported to be recovering at a local hospital, and thankfully, a senseless tragedy was avoided by the narrowest of margins.

One of the disturbing changes I've seen take place over the years regarding guns is the drastic shift towards a "gun culture". It has been thirty years since I first carried a firearm for a living and my views have not changed much since. Being armed was a tremendous responsibility as well as a burden at times. Shooting was not my hobby, I went to the range to train. My gun was not a shiny new toy but a deadly weapon and a tool of my trade. Now it seems that guns are viewed quite differently by some. People show off their new Glock like they just picked up the latest iPhone. I personally know a woman who has a pink one, and no, I don't mean the phone. When this topic comes up for debate, some will say, "Well, what's the harm?". They're all quick to point out that guns are not toys, but how are people to differentiate if we continue to package them and treat them as such.

A friend recently purchased a new Sig Sauer handgun, and I couldn't help but notice the "SIG" sticker that came with it proudly displayed on the back of his truck. It was gone the next time I saw him after I had casually mentioned that someone might find that an enticement to break and enter his vehicle. Living in Florida, I know many people who legally carry a gun. How do I know that they carry a gun? It's not due to my keen observational abilities, they tell me so. Some even show me that they are carrying even though I never asked. When I have carried a gun, nobody knew about it. I didn't tell anyone, and I certainly never showed anyone.

One of the things about carrying a firearm that I find most concerning is that it changes the overall mindset of an individual. Carrying a firearm will not magically make someone tougher or braver. I have often said that a wimp with a gun is a very dangerous thing. Armed or not, your objective should always be to avoid a dangerous situation, leaving confrontation as a last and unavoidable resort. There is nothing wrong with fleeing if that is a viable option, but unfortunately, the decision-making process sometimes changes when a person becomes *armed*. People will often conduct themselves differently if they are carrying a gun. Case in point, the shooting of teenager Trayvon Martin by neighborhood watch volunteer George Zimmerman. Martin was walking through the gated community where he was staying in Sanford, Florida in 2012. Zimmerman, who was inside his vehicle at the time, observed Martin and called the police to report a "suspicious person" and to request that a patrol car be sent out. Zimmerman, who later stated that he believed Martin would be gone by the time the police arrived, exited his vehicle and confronted him. What happened next is something that only George Zimmerman knows for sure.

An altercation ensued and resulted in Zimmerman fatally shooting Martin with his 9mm Kel-Tec handgun.

George Zimmerman was tried and ultimately found not guilty, citing self-defense. The case was widely publicized and fiercely debated. Like many, I have my own opinions about the case and subsequent outcome of the trial, but I am not going to delve into that subject here. I only bring up this case to illustrate one very specific point. Regardless of what exactly took place during that altercation, it is my belief that Zimmerman's decision-making process was changed by the fact that he was armed. I believe that George Zimmerman was emboldened by the fact that he had a gun and compelled to get out of his vehicle to confront Martin, who was unarmed and as it turns out, simply returning home from a convenience store where he had bought some candy. What would Zimmerman have chosen to do if he was not carrying a gun? Would he have still gotten out of the car or would he have waited and observed until law enforcement arrived? We will never know how things might have played out differently, but if he had made a different choice, the altercation may have never taken place, and a teenage boy might still be alive today.

Aside from the shift in thinking that can take place when someone straps on a gun, there is often the misconception that you will instantly become safer by owning or carrying a firearm. In some cases, the opposite is true. A weapon can be taken from you if you are not thoroughly prepared to not only use it but to also protect it. You should keep in mind that your gun may be the only one in the room, and if you are unable to retain possession of it, you may wind up arming an otherwise unarmed assailant. While actors make killing look so easy, truth be told, your typical soccer mom or real estate agent for that matter, does not suddenly become Jason Bourne when a situation turns deadly. Being mentally as well as physically prepared is essential. The gun on your hip or in your purse is not what will ultimately save your life, it is the intelligence of the person behind the weapon.

Without wading too far into the subject of self-defense and the legalities of using deadly force, there is one very important point that I would like to make. Being legally authorized to carry a weapon does not mean that you are deputized as a law enforcement officer. The gun that you carry is intended for self-defense purposes. That means to defend yourself or another from death or grave bodily injury. Additionally, that threat must be "imminent".

In a perfect example of what not to do, I will share with you the story of a Good Samaritan in Houston, Texas. He pulled up to a gas station one night where he became aware that another customer was being car-jacked. The "Samaritan" exited his vehicle with a handgun and opened fire. The suspects escaped, but he did hit the car-jacking victim, who survived even though he was shot in the head. The shooter then gathered up his shell casings and fled the scene. I can't say for sure what the mindset of this individual was as he is still at large, but I think it's safe to say that he had good intentions when he intervened. In my humble opinion, the biggest flaw with the concept of a "good guy with a gun" is that a great many of them are grossly incompetent.

If you do decide to carry a handgun, please make that decision with a great deal of forethought and deliberation. Getting the proper legal permit is only the beginning. There is a vast difference between being legally qualified to carry a gun, and being truly qualified. Just like obtaining your real estate license was a starting point, the same holds true for a carry permit. It is the beginning of your education, not the end. Here in Florida, concealed carry training consists of four hours of classroom followed by range time. That range time can consist of firing one round at a target. That's not a typo. ONE bullet. It's akin to allowing someone to fly a jet once they have successfully folded a sheet of paper into an airplane. Some courses are better than others and I recommend the ones that are sponsored and taught by law enforcement.

In the end, I can't tell you whether or not you should carry a gun, but I hope I have done my part and given you an awful lot to think about. It is a decision that only you can make. If you do decide that you want to arm yourself, I sincerely hope that you will take that responsibility very seriously. If you feel that a handgun is not the right defensive solution for you, I will discuss a very effective alternative in the coming pages.

BY THE NUMBERS

39,773 - The number of gun related deaths in the United States in 2017. It's the highest number reported since the prior record was set in 1993.

14,542 - The number of gun related homicides in 2017, the highest yearly total since the 1990s.

23,854 - The number of gun related suicides in 2017.

12.2 - The number of gun deaths per 100,000 people in 2017, surpassing the number of deaths from automobile accidents for the first time.

Source: The Center for Disease Control

RED HOT CHILI PEPPERS 20

"ATTEN-TION!" The Senior Tactical Officer barked.

In one swift motion, the group of 33 Police Academy cadets snapped in sync, bolt upright, thumbs and forefingers pinching the out-seam of their crisply pressed trousers. We looked sharp, standing there in the morning sun, and a far cry from where our original group of 50 hopefuls had begun. The early stages of our training focused more on breaking us down and inflicting pain and stress, whereas now we were in the home stretch, the finish line clearly in sight. From here on out, our daily activities would be devoted to education and practical training, although our "T.O."s would still throw in a little torture from time to time, if only to remind us that we weren't quite cops just yet. We had certainly come a long way. Our days at the academy were becoming much more interesting and dare I say, enjoyable. Once feeling beaten down and uncertain, we had transformed into a confident and poised group of cadets. The 88th session of the San Bernardino County Sheriff's Academy was nearly a finished product.

"You have been extensively trained in the use of various weapons." the Sergeant said. "Handgun, shotgun, baton..."

We listened intently as he told us of the morning's agenda. "Today, you will be instructed in the proper use of chemical agents and gain a comprehensive understanding of this weapon's effectiveness."

It sounded pretty cool, at least that's what I thought to myself. That opinion changed after a couple of hours with the realization of what "an understanding of the weapon's effectiveness" actually meant.

Our first contact with chemical Mace occurred when it was applied to our cheeks by a Tactical Officer, just below the right eye. It was the first of three exposures that morning, each followed by an hour-long classroom session where we were lectured on I have no idea what. We were not allowed to touch our face and were required to sit in silence at our desks, eyes front. Silence presumably meant without speaking since the constant chorus of coughs, sniffles, and wheezes was certainly unavoidable.

Now keep in mind that the year was 1987, so Mace was the chemical agent of choice in the law enforcement community and had not yet been replaced by the now popular pepper spray. Often confused, the two have much in common, with the primary difference being the active ingredient. Mace is a combination of CN gas (phenacyl chloride) suspended in a chemical solvent, whereas pepper spray utilizes OC gas (oleoresin capsicum), a derivative of chili peppers, as the prime component. Both products are delivered by way of an aerosol propellant. They will irritate and burn the skin on contact, and inflame the membranes of the eyes, nose, lungs, and throat, making it difficult to breathe and function in general. Because of it's less toxic side effects as well as its superior effectiveness, pepper spray has become the most common self-defense spray in use today.

Some years later, I was inadvertently exposed to pepper spray and can confirm that it is just as effective as its predecessor. Aside from being incredibly irritating, it can also cause some degree of temporary blindness. You should not underestimate the potency of pepper spray and its value as a defensive weapon. If you have ever cut up Jalapenos or similar type peppers in your kitchen and unwittingly touched your eyes or face, you have experienced a small sample of the effects of capsicum.

As I'm sure you have guessed, I survived my chemical Mace training at the police academy and suffered no lasting effects. Within an hour of exposure, the symptoms had diminished and we were all pretty much back to normal. The exercise served multiple purposes, all of which were invaluable. We experienced first hand the effects of a chemical agent and also came to understand that despite how horrible it made us feel, the discomfort was temporary and we would recover from it. That knowledge helped us to function in a controlled environment while exposed to Mace so that we would be less likely to panic if we accidentally came in contact with it in the field.

Police Officers are often exposed to chemical spray when using it on a suspect so remaining calm and collected during the confrontation is essential. I can recall talking with my fellow trainees over lunch, laughing and joking about how we all felt like we were experiencing something worse than what was intended, as if we each had some rare and unexpected reaction. It really just felt that lousy, but now all was well and we had survived. Our Mace training was completed, another hurdle cleared on our way to graduation. The afternoon session would certainly be a piece of cake after all we had endured that morning. The blackboard only said "Afternoon-CS training". It turned out that "CS" is the commonly used name for tear gas.

You may have sensed from the previous chapter that I am very hesitant to endorse the carrying of a firearm for self-defense purposes. The risks and potentially devastating consequences are difficult to reconcile. On the other hand, in my opinion, pepper spray is a virtual no-brainer. Used properly, it is an excellent choice to thwart a would-be attacker, and in many ways has an advantage over deadly force. It is easy to obtain, simple to use, and does not involve the extreme life or death decisions that one must make in a matter of mere seconds.

I strongly believe that the hesitation that inevitably occurs when deciding to fire a gun is greatly reduced when using a non-lethal weapon. Remember, there is no shoot to wound option in the real world when it comes to guns. The decision is only shoot-don't shoot. Pepper spray is an excellent choice to deter and incapacitate an assailant and offers you an opportunity to escape without the grave consequences of using a firearm. It is also worth mentioning that the risks involved with owning, transporting, and storing pepper spray are far less than those associated with handgun ownership. If someone manages to take the weapon and use it against you, it will not be pleasant, but you will survive. If it should be lost, stolen, or otherwise fall into the wrong hands, it will not be used to kill a police officer or rob a convenience store.

Most importantly, if a child should ever get his or her hands on your pepper spray, the dangers are drastically reduced. Obviously, this does not excuse you from exercising sound judgment and responsible behavior. Pepper spray is a weapon and should still be safeguarded as such. Additionally, the legalities of owning and carrying pepper spray or any other chemical agent must be thoroughly investigated to ensure that you are in compliance with all state and local laws. Regulation of pepper spray has eased over the past few years but possession is still commonly limited to a small quantity to avoid it being used to incapacitate a large group of people. Similarly, it may be legal to carry but banned in certain areas such as government buildings, airports, etc. Again, research the rules that apply before purchasing or carrying pepper spray.

If you decide to carry such a weapon, read the literature that is provided with the product as directions for use vary by manufacturer. You should purchase pepper spray that is easy to use and has a guard over the trigger to avoid accidental discharge while in a purse or pocket. The guard, as well as a molded grip, helps to ensure that it is pointed away from you when used. You should carry it in an easily accessible location. This can include a coat pocket, purse, on a belt clip or keychain. More importantly, you should always carry it in the same place. An attacker will not pause while you try to remember where you left your pepper spray. Many products are quite small in size, primarily to comply with local laws regarding limitation of the amount that is legal to possess. These small sized canisters fit nicely and discreetly in the palm of your hand if you should be in a situation where you are feeling uneasy.

Using pepper spray is fairly simple, just point and shoot. You should extend your arm slightly to avoid being exposed to the agent yourself, but not so far as to make it easy for the assailant to grab a hold of it. Most types have ranges of 6-10 feet so it is not necessary to be close to your target. Back away as you spray as the product may splash backward and you will want to avoid potentially being affected yourself.

The term "spray" is actually a bit misleading as pepper spray usually exits the canister in a concentrated stream and can be aimed with a fair degree of accuracy. Don't just give him a little spritz and wait to see if it works. Aim for the face and fire a good two or three-second burst. It only takes a short time for the effects to kick in, about three seconds. At this point, you should be withdrawing as your ultimate objective is to buy time to leave the area, but keep the pepper spray trained on your target's face and ready to give him a second burst if he should begin to advance. If he does, don't hesitate to hose him down. If you would like to see a visual demonstration of the proper use of pepper spray, a video can be found on my Facebook page.

THE FOX AND THE OLD LION 21

An old Lion, whose teeth and claws were so worn that it was not so easy for him to get food as in his younger days, pretended that he was sick. He took care to let all his neighbors know about it, and then lay down in his cave to wait for visitors. And when they came to offer him their sympathy, he ate them up one by one.

The Fox came too, but he was very cautious about it. Standing at a safe distance from the cave, he inquired politely after the Lion's health. The Lion replied that he was very ill indeed, and asked the Fox to step in for a moment. But Master Fox very wisely stayed outside, thanking the Lion very kindly for the invitation.

"I should be glad to do as you ask," he added, "but I have noticed that there are many footprints leading into your cave and none coming out. Pray tell me, how do your visitors find their way out again?"

The story above was written by Aesop, a Greek storyteller credited with a number of yarns collectively known as "Aesop's Fables". His tales are short and are often characterized by animals that speak. They include sometimes subtle wisdom and have been interpreted in various ways throughout the years. I like to think of the meaning of "The Fox and the Old Lion" in this way. While the lion was clever and used deception to lure his prey, the fox was clever as well and learned from the misfortune of those who had gone before him.

While it is not difficult to take heed of the tragic accounts of people who have fallen victim to violence, in the realm of safety and security, the tales of success are seldom told. There are occasional stories of close calls and of those who narrowly escaped peril, but for the most part, it's difficult to measure the effectiveness of the precautions that any given person might take. Simply put, many of the safety measures that we practice are preemptive, and the true success of those efforts are never really known.

For a person in my field, that can sometimes make safety and security a tough sell. It is my sincere hope that you will take what you have learned in this book and not only make it a part of your career but also a part of your everyday life. That said, I would like to pose to you this hypothetical question. Imagine that we could leap forward in time, several years into the future, or even decades perhaps, and find ourselves at your retirement party. Assuming that you had in fact been my star pupil (as I know you will be), and followed my recommendations to the letter, imagine that I was to ask you if the safety measures that you had so diligently employed for all these years had been at all successful. Aside from the obvious fact that you had arrived at the end of your career unscathed, chances are that your truthful answer would be "I really don't know".

Most people are able to measure the successfulness of their respective careers by way of achievement and accomplishment. As a real estate agent, I'm sure you can evaluate the merits of your professional endeavors in several different ways. Perhaps you have achieved the status of "multi-million dollar producer" or received awards or accolades during the course of your career. Maybe you look at it from a standpoint of dollars and cents and measure your success by way of profitability. For the security specialist, effectiveness is often much more difficult to quantify for the simple reason that it is considered a great success when literally, nothing happens. For me personally, I look at it as a numbers game. I know in my heart of hearts that the more people who hear this message, the greater the likelihood that it will inevitably save some of them from harm.

If you're like most people, you take steps to protect yourself every single day without really giving it much thought. I'll bet that you lock the doors to your house when you go to bed at night and again when you leave in the morning. You probably lock your car when you arrive at work as well. Perhaps you have installed an alarm system in your home or added some motion sensor lights on the exterior. All of these security measures make good common sense, and it would be hard to argue otherwise, but chances are that you have no idea if they are at all effective. While you may have known that your neighbor's house was burglarized last summer, what you didn't know was that the burglar had entered your backyard first, only to be deterred by the glare of that annoying security light. It was also common knowledge around the office that items were stolen from your co-worker's car, but you were totally unaware of the fact that the thief had tried every car door in the lot, including yours, before finally hitting the jackpot.

All of the precautions listed above, and many others I'm sure, are things that you do automatically, and you probably don't feel overly inconvenienced by them either. Repetition leads to habit, and those habits become second nature. I can assure you that the methods outlined in this book, with a little repetition, will become habit and in time you will find yourself doing them without much thought at all. Think back to when you first received your learner's permit and began to drive. Remember all of the focus and concentration that was put into simply maneuvering the car around an empty parking lot? Anything can become intuitive if you simply apply yourself and give it some conscious effort in the early going.

If you commit to making personal safety a part of your everyday life, it will become one of the many things that you do instinctively and without giving it a second thought. You must begin by being mindful of your own safety and by keeping this topic at the forefront of the conversation. It is important to keep this discussion going and the most effective way to do so is by simply sharing. Share what you know, and share what you have learned. The best way to remember is to be reminded. "Be safe" should not just be a catchphrase. Take stock in your own well being and encourage others to do the same. In short, pass it on. Ensure that this becomes as important to your colleagues as it is to you. Any endeavor is easier to accomplish if you enlist the help of your friends. Your safety should not just be a part of your career, it should be a part of your office culture and your everyday life.

When I say share, I don't mean it figuratively. Literally, share this book. Now that you are finished, share it, lend it, give it away to a fellow agent and encourage them to pass it on when they are finished. Perhaps you could donate your copy to the office's learning library. As a writer, of course I would love to sell a million copies of this book, but I will let you in on a little secret. There's no money in writing security books. If you are looking for the fast track to fame and fortune, this is definitely not the ticket. I would much rather sell one copy of this book that got passed around the office and read by every single agent than to sell a hundred that were never opened.

Additionally, feel free to share with me. I am accessible via social media at www.facebook.com/prospectorpredator. There you will find my email address as well as links to additional content in both written and video format. I will continue to strive towards offering current and hopefully compelling information on safety and security for real estate agents. I would welcome your input and ideas as well as hearing about your own personal experiences. Several of the methods outlined on these pages were a direct result of the contributions of working real estate professionals.

As our journey draws to a close, I'd like to think that I've provided you with a set of tools, that if used properly, will ultimately keep you safe from harm. But if I am going to be completely honest, I must tell you that the most effective self-protection tools are the ones that you already possess. They have been in your possession all along and at your disposal since long before you opened this book. They just had to be taken out and dusted off a bit. Far more powerful than any firearm or martial arts technique, your God-given intellect and good old fashioned common sense remain your best and most reliable weapons to avoid falling victim to crime. Use them wisely. Be present in the moment, aware of your surroundings, and above all else, trust your instincts.

GARY VAN CLIEF attended the San Bernardino County Sheriff's Academy in Southern California, graduating in 1987. His training continued with International Diplomatic Security of Los Angeles. In the late 1980s and early '90s he was responsible for the security of one of America's most prominent individuals and his family, working and traveling as part of a close protection detail. He has worked as a Security Consultant and has written and spoken on matters of safety and security spanning over 25 years.

www.ingramcontent.com/pod-product-compliance
Lightning Source LLC
Chambersburg PA
CBHW031839170526
45157CB00001B/364